ITHACA FARMERS MARKET

ITHACA FARMERS MARKET

A Seasonal Guide and Cookbook
Celebrating the Market's First 50 Years

MICHAEL TURBACK
IZZY LECEK

NORTH COUNTRY BOOKS

An imprint of Globe Pequot, the trade division of
The Rowman & Littlefield Publishing Group, Inc.
4501 Forbes Blvd., Ste. 200
Lanham, MD 20706
www.rowman.com

Distributed by NATIONAL BOOK NETWORK

British Library Cataloguing in Publication Information Available

Library of Congress Cataloging-in-Publication Data

Names: Turback, Michael, author. | Lecek, Izzy, author.
Title: Ithaca Farmers Market : a seasonal guide and cookbook celebrating the market's first 50 years / Michael Turback, Izzy Lecek.
Description: Lanham, MD : North Country, [2024] | Includes index. | Summary: "Celebrating a historic milestone at the Market's current Pavilion location, Ithaca Farmers Market captures the energy and history of the market through colorful narratives, vivid historical and contemporary photos, detailed recipes, and helpful shopping and prep guides"— Provided by publisher.
Identifiers: LCCN 2023046385 (print) | LCCN 2023046386 (ebook) | ISBN 9781493078370 (cloth) | ISBN 9781493078387 (epub)
Subjects: LCSH: Cooking, American. | Ithaca Farmers Market (Ithaca, New York)—History. | Local foods—Ithaca—New York. | Seasonal cooking. | LCGFT: Cookbooks.
Classification: LCC TX715 .T9015 2024 (print) | LCC TX715 (ebook) | DDC 641.59747/71—dc23/eng/20231220
LC record available at https://lccn.loc.gov/2023046385
LC ebook record available at https://lccn.loc.gov/2023046386

∞™ The paper used in this publication meets the minimum requirements of American National Standard for Information Sciences—Permanence of Paper for Printed Library Materials, ANSI/NISO Z39.48-1992

To Jan Rhodes Norman

Jan has championed the locality of Ithaca, not only with her passion, dedication, leadership, and long service to the farmers market, but also as a founding member of Greenstar Co-op, as cofounder of Local First Ithaca, and as a fearless local activist.

CONTENTS

SUMMER

WINTER

INTRODUCTION

*I go to the local farmers
market and decide on
what to cook, depending
on what I find.*

—JACQUES PÉPIN,
CHEF AND CULINARY EDUCATOR

Nearly every Saturday and Sunday morning at Steamboat Landing, you will see the faithful browsing our local market in search of the freshest and most beautiful produce, filling bags and baskets with fixings for the week's home meals, encouraging farmers and growers to extend their culinary reach. More than half a century, many of us have adapted and translated our cooking to locally inspired meals that make delicious use of the market bounty.

A far cry from the ragtag brigade selling off the backs of pickup trucks in 1973, today's bustling pavilion hosts an array of social ventures, meeting the demand for fresh, locally grown vegetables and fruits, meat from pastured animals, and handcrafted wines and ciders. Farmers and growers engage in sustainable practices to produce healthy food for those of us who are concerned with not just what we eat, but how and where it's produced. We've caught on to the fact that eating locally is better for our health, the environment, and the economy.

The Ithaca Farmers Market has reduced the distance between a farmer's field and our dinner plates to thirty miles or less and in the process has become one of the most influential community enterprises, consistently named among the top five farmers markets in the country.

Ithaca Farmers Market Cookbook, published in 2010, focused on vendors, told their stories, and offered an eclectic mix of recipes based on their specialties. The book came to the attention of chef and "slow food" activist Alice Waters, who wrote, "Buying from farmers markets not only promotes edible education for children and adults alike, but also stabilizes a local economy and introduces people to a variety of culinary cultures. With delicious recipes and charming stories, *Ithaca Farmers Market Cookbook* demonstrates the importance of fresh, seasonal and sustainable ingredients."

This follow-up book celebrates a significant milestone of our beloved local institution with stories, photos, and recipes that channel both vendors and shoppers, capturing the bursting energy of the market pavilion and documenting the evolution of the market from its modest beginnings to its importance as a vital community and regional asset.

Folks who have been in Ithaca a long time will find a particularly fruitful trail of breadcrumbs, a bit of history and reintroduction to characters who made it a social and cultural mainstay. Throughout its fifty-year history, the Ithaca Farmers Market has become a gathering place where strangers become friends, where shoppers get to know the farmers and what they do to feed us.

In addition to glimpses of nostalgia, this is a practical guide to the delicious possibilities of cooking with local produce at the height of flavor and freshness throughout the growing seasons—from spring to early summer to midsummer to the bursting harvest of late summer, then ebbing into fall and winter, taking the reader/shopper on a year-round culinary tour of the calendar. The succession of crops means that every season at the market brings a new riot of color, taste, and texture.

Valuable, usable advice about shopping in accordance with rhythms of our growing seasons reconnects marketgoers with the cycles of nature in our farms and fields, offering recipes for fresh and delicious dishes made with each season's star ingredients.

Shopping at our local market makes us feel more connected to the community. Getting closer to our food helps us get a bit closer to each other. Eating in tune with the seasons makes us feel more connected to the earth.

Eating is an agricultural act.

—WENDELL BERRY,

POET AND FARMER

To Market, to Market

Essence of Summer

Market Milestone

Rainbow of Carrots

Bounty of Blueberries

Picked Peppers

Pavilion at High Noon

Pavilion at High Noon

First Vegetable of Spring

Make a Beeline to Waid's

Karen Purcell and David Slattery, Picaflor Farm, Member since 2022

Japan's Gift to the Market

Beyond Organic Root Vegetables
from Sabol's Farm

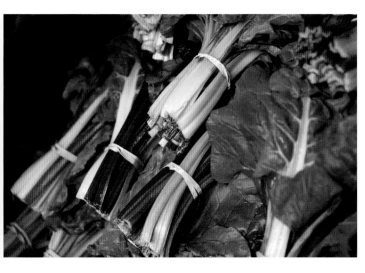

Eat Your Colors

Lucy and Greta Garrison-Clauson, Stick and Stone Farm, Member since 1996

Madi and Chuck Alridge, Jasper Meadows Farm, Member since 2022

Welcome to the Market

Community Gathering Place

Music of the Market

Kuukua Yomekpe, Asempe Kitchen, Member since 2022

Mary and Rachel McGarry-Newman, Buried Treasures Organic Farm, Member since 2009

Jan Rhodes Norman, Silk Oak, Member since 1996

Herbs, the Unsung Hero of the Season

*Angel Stillions, Blackduck
Cidery/Daring Drake Farm,
Member since 2008*

Christina Neumann, Osakaya, Member since 1994

Italian Heirloom Onions, the Color of Red Wine

Stop and Smell the Garlic

Michael Burns, Cayuta Sun Farm, Member since 2015

Looking Radish-ing

Tonic for Mind and Body

Rob Golkowski, Old Chatham Creamery, Member since 2022

Handcrafted Popcorn

Richard Sabol, Sabol's Farm, Member since 1987

Livin' La Vida Vodka

Cheryl Barton, Bellwether Hard Cider, Member since 2000

Carolina Hassett, Carolina Perez Designs, Member since 1992

Steven Daughhetee, New York Cider Company, Member since 2018

Christi A. Sobel, Member since 2001

Roll out the Pumpkins

The Ultimate Slushie

SPRING

It is Spring again. The earth is like a child that knows poems by heart.

—Rainer Maria Rilke

BEVERAGES AND COCKTAILS

"Liberty Spy" Sparkling Cider French 75

MAKES 1 DRINK

The term bellwether comes from an age-old practice in sheepherding of putting a bell on the sheep that leads the flock. Bellwethers now refer to people who take the lead, stick their necks out, and start a movement. In 1996, Bill and Cheryl Barton became leading figures in the revival of cidermaking in the region with an ambitious start-up they appropriately called Bellwether Hard Cider.

Members of the market since 2000, the Bartons' mainstays include Liberty Spy, a sparkling cider crafted from a blend of Liberty and Northern Spy apples (both native New York varieties). Perfectly balanced between sweet and dry, the effervescent cider replaces champagne in the classic French 75, a cocktail named for the fast-firing 75-millimeter field gun utilized by the French during World War I.

1½ ounces gin
½ ounce fresh lemon juice
Bellwether Liberty Spy Sparkling
 Cider, chilled

1. Combine gin and lemon juice in a mixing glass filled with cracked ice.

2. Shake vigorously and strain into a coupe or flute.

3. Top up with the sparkling cider.

Rhubarb Gin Sour

MAKES 1 DRINK

This seasonal gin sour showcases rhubarb, arriving at the market in early spring from Mandeville Farm in Spencer. Treated as a fruit but technically a vegetable, rhubarb adds its unique sweet-tart flavor and color to the floral notes of gin and the tartness of lemon, a refreshing way to toast the arrival of the queen of seasons. The first shake, or "dry shake," gives the cocktail a lovely foam and brilliant mouthfeel.

2 ounces gin
1 ounce rhubarb simple syrup*
1 ounce fresh lemon juice
1 egg white
mint sprig

1. Combine gin, rhubarb simple syrup, lemon juice, and egg white into a mixing glass.

2. Dry shake for one to two minutes until egg white is fully emulsified.

3. Add cracked ice to the shaker and shake again for 30 seconds.

4. Strain into a chilled coupe glass and garnish with the mint sprig.

*To make rhubarb simple syrup:

1 cup sugar
1 cup water
2 cups chopped Mandeville Farm rhubarb

1. Place ingredients in a small saucepan over medium-high heat. Bring to a boil while stirring constantly.

2. Remove from the heat and allow the mixture to steep for at least 1 hour. Strain rhubarb pieces by pouring over a strainer into a sealable container. Keep cool until ready to use.

Wildflower Honey "Bee's Knees"

MAKES 1 DRINK

Duane Waid, an artisan honey producer for nearly half a century, is single-handedly responsible for creating a multitude of local honey snobs. He joined the market in 1977, selling honeys that reflect the terroir of berry fields, apple orchards, and wide meadows of wildflowers in between Cayuga and Seneca Lakes. Unlike commercial, large-scale producers who refine and filter their honey so that it is brilliantly clear and heat it above 140 degrees to prevent crystallization, Waid's honeys are processed under low temperature and strained through fine-weave cloth to retain pollen and healthful enzymes.

Mr. Waid passed the torch to Greg Reynolds (of Glenwood Farms), who now keeps about one hundred colonies of bees and produces between ten thousand and fifteen thousand pounds of honey each year. Among his extraordinary spring honeys, the lighter variety "wildflower" becomes the silky sweetener in a vintage refresher, the original recipe credited to bartender Frank Meier, who plied his trade at the Hôtel Ritz in Paris during the 1920s.

2 ounces gin
¾ ounce fresh lemon juice
¾ ounce honey syrup*
lemon peel

1. Combine liquid ingredients in a mixing glass filled with cracked ice.

2. Shake vigorously and strain into a chilled cocktail glass.

3. Express lemon peel over the surface and drop into the glass.

*To make honey syrup:

1. Combine 2 ounces Waid's Apiaries wildflower honey with 1 ounce hot water in a sealed container. Shake until combined.

2. Allow to cool.

Makes enough syrup for 4 drinks.

SALADS AND SMALL PLATES

Creamy Mashed Potatoes with Sorrel

MAKES 4 SERVINGS

Both an herb and a leafy green, fiddle-shaped sorrel leaves taste best and are most tender when picked as baby leaves, a couple of inches long. The pronounced tartness of sorrel brightens and enlivens this potato side dish.

Tim and Noelia Springston inherited the patch of sorrel when they purchased the land for Oxbow Farm two decades ago. They harvest that perennial patch sparingly to allow the plants to recover and thrive.

4 Sabol's Farm Keuka Gold potatoes, peeled and cut into 1-inch chunks
4 ounces Oxbow Farm sorrel leaves, washed
2 tablespoons unsalted butter
½ cup heavy cream
kosher salt
freshly ground black pepper

1. Add potatoes to a pot of cold water. Boil until tender.

2. Meanwhile, cut the sorrel leaves into thin strips. Heat butter in a frying pan and add the sorrel. Stir over low heat until wilted, about 2 minutes. Stir in the cream. Remove from heat and set aside.

3. Mash the potatoes. Stir in the sorrel. Season with salt and pepper to taste.

4. Transfer to a warmed serving bowl and pass, family style, around the table.

Garlic Greens on Sourdough Toast

MAKES 6 SERVINGS

Garlic green stalks are pulled by growers while still immature, before garlic bulbs have a chance to fully form cloves. They show up at the market after growers thin the fields to make space for maturing, "heading" bulbs.

To prepare, simply trim off the very bottom part (the bulb with roots) and use both the white and green parts of the stalk to make piquant butter spread for toast, an excellent nibble with drinks.

¼ cup Six Circles Farm garlic green stalks, chopped
¾ stick unsalted butter, softened
¼ cup freshly grated Parmesan cheese
1 tablespoon minced chives
pinch of sea salt
pinch of freshly ground black pepper
6 slices Wide Awake Bakery sourdough bread

1. In a small bowl, stir together garlic greens, butter, cheese, chives, salt, and pepper.

2. Heat the broiler. Place the bread slices on a baking sheet and toast, then flip and toast the other side.

3. Spread toast slices with the garlic greens butter. Broil buttered toast until browned on top, about 1 to 2 minutes.

4. Arrange toast on a serving platter and pass family style around the table.

Hakurei Turnip Salad with Arugula and Easter Egg Radishes

MAKES 4 SERVINGS

West Haven Farm has been feeding certified organic fruits and vegetables to marketgoers since 1995. Started by John and Jen Bokaer-Smith, the ten-acre farm on the land of EcoVillage is now in the hands of Carlos Aguilera and Lorena Mendoza. One of the farm's most interesting crops, the Hakurei turnip, is a Japanese variety root vegetable with a mild flavor, natural sweetness, and a juicy, crunchy texture. It's sometimes referred to as a salad turnip because of its delicious raw flavor, partnering in this dish with arugula and radishes.

Easter Egg radishes from Buried Treasures Organic Farm are a blend of multiple varieties, planted together to create a multicolored crop of pink, white, red, and purple radishes.

The dressing calls for honey from Bright Raven Apiary in Jacksonville. Spring honey gets its sweet start by bees who wild forage for nectar and pollen from maple, dandelion, willow, fruit trees, rose hips, wild brambles, black locust, and basswood flowers on the farm.

4 teaspoons red wine vinegar
2 teaspoons Bright Raven Apiary
   Spring Bloom honey
¼ cup extra-virgin olive oil
3 or 4 West Haven Farm Hakurei
   turnips, peeled
8 cups arugula, chopped
4 Buried Treasures Organic Farm
   Easter Egg radishes, sliced thin
sea salt
freshly ground black pepper

1. In a small bowl, whisk together the vinegar, honey, and olive oil.

2. Using a mandoline or sharp knife, shave the turnips into paper-thin rounds.

3. In a large bowl, combine turnips, arugula, and radishes. Toss with the dressing. Season with salt and pepper to taste.

4. To serve, divide the salad among 4 chilled plates.

Herb Biscuits with Salted Honey Butter

MAKES 1 DOZEN BISCUITS

Karen Purcell was born and raised in Chile, South America, earned degrees at Cornell and NYU, and worked at the Cornell Lab of Ornithology before starting Picaflor Farm in Danby. (Picaflor means "hummingbird" in Chilean Spanish.)

The Picaflor family of bees visits maple, basswood, peach, apple flowers, lilacs, magnolia, asparagus flowers, and coltsfoot near the farm, producing the nectar that becomes spring honey. The lush combination of honey and butter is elevated with a kiss of flaky sea salt, the ultimate topping for the light-as-air biscuits served with breakfast or evening tea.

2 cups all-purpose flour

1 teaspoon sea salt

1 teaspoon sugar

1 tablespoon baking powder

1 tablespoon chopped fresh basil

7 tablespoons unsalted butter, cold, cut into ¼-inch pieces

¾ cup Crosswinds Creamery milk

salted honey butter*

1. Preheat oven to 425 degrees F. Line a baking sheet with parchment paper.

2. In a large bowl, combine flour, salt, sugar, baking powder, and basil. Whisk to combine.

3. Add butter to flour with a pastry cutter; cut butter into dough the size of peas.

4. Add milk to the bowl and stir until a dough forms.

5. Transfer dough to a lightly floured surface. Roll dough out to ¾-inch thick. Use a 3-inch biscuit cutter to cut out biscuits. Transfer biscuits to the prepared baking sheet.

6. Bake until golden, about 15 minutes. Remove from oven.

7. Serve warm with the honey butter. Store any leftover biscuits, well wrapped, at room temperature for several days. Freeze for longer storage.

*For the salted honey butter:

1 stick unsalted butter, at room temperature

3 tablespoons Picaflor Farm spring honey

1 tablespoon Maldon sea salt flakes

1. Using a handheld mixer, whip butter and honey until smooth and fluffy.

2. Gradually fold in salt flakes with a spatula.

Makes 1 cup

Kale Raab with Chile and Lemon

MAKES 4 SERVINGS

Kale blossoms, the bolting tops of the plant, are harvested from overwintering kale while the buds are still intact and before the plant can fully bloom. Available at the market for a slightly truncated season, quick-cooking raab, with the heat of red pepper and the tartness of lemon, is a transient treat. For that matter, use it to top pasta, rice, mashed potatoes, or soba noodles.

1 pound West Haven Farm kale raab
2 to 4 tablespoons extra-virgin olive oil
¼ teaspoon crushed red pepper flakes
juice of 1 lemon
kosher salt
freshly ground black pepper

1. Remove leaves from kale raab stalk and chop into bite-sized pieces.

2. Heat olive oil in a saute pan over medium heat.

3. Saute the kale raab in the hot oil, stirring occasionally. Sprinkle red pepper flakes over top and cook, about 3 to 4 minutes, or until the raab is tender. Remove from heat.

4. Transfer to a warmed serving bowl, stir in lemon juice, season with salt and pepper to taste, and pass family style around the table.

"No Time to Cook" Asparagus

MAKES 4 SERVINGS

The Romans had a saying when they wanted something done quickly. "Do it," they said, "in less time than it takes to cook asparagus." One of the quickest and easiest ways to prepare fresh asparagus is to simply blanch the spears for a couple of minutes and toss them with freshly grated Parmesan cheese, olive oil, and lemon zest.

Asparagus is one of the most sought-after vegetables at the spring market. They go only to the first shoppers, so plan to arrive early to get the tender, just-harvested shoots. You'll find different lengths and thicknesses on display. Look for thin stalks at the Mandeville Farm stand.

1 pound Mandeville Farm pencil-thin
    asparagus spears
2 tablespoons extra-virgin olive oil
2 tablespoons freshly grated
    Parmesan cheese
1 teaspoon lemon zest
kosher salt
freshly cracked black pepper

1. Rinse asparagus thoroughly. Trim any tough bottoms and discard.

2. Fill a large saucepan with 1 inch of lightly salted water. Bring to a boil.

3. Add the asparagus, cover and boil until bright green and crisp-tender, about 3 to 5 minutes.

4. Drain the hot water. Toss asparagus with olive oil, Parmesan, and lemon zest.

5. Transfer to a warmed serving plate, season with salt and pepper to taste, and pass family style around the table.

Pak Choi with Garlic and Oyster Sauce

MAKES 4 SERVINGS

It takes extra care to grow pak choi (also called pok choi, bok choy, or Chinese celery cabbage), particularly at a farm like Oxbow, where vegetables are lovingly grown without the use of pesticides. To capture the true essence of this seasonal crop, Tim and Noelia Springston start pak choi as seeds in February, nurturing them until they are ready to be transplanted in March. With careful cultivation, they are typically brought to the market by the second week of April, at their absolute peak of flavor and texture.

3 tablespoons oyster sauce
1 tablespoon soy sauce
2 tablespoons rice vinegar
1 tablespoon extra-virgin olive oil
1 tablespoon minced garlic
1½ pounds Oxbow Farm pak choi, washed, ends trimmed
2 tablespoons water

1. Combine oyster sauce, soy sauce, and rice vinegar in a bowl and set aside.

2. Heat oil in a skillet or wok set over high heat. Add garlic and pak choi and stir-fry for 2 minutes. Add 2 tablespoons of water to the skillet or wok, cover and allow to cook for 2 minutes more, until pak choi is tender but still vibrant. Remove from heat.

3. Transfer to a warmed serving platter. Drizzle the reserved sauce over the greens and pass family style around the table.

Ramp Butter

Sometimes called spring onions, ramps are earthy and savory, not quite as potent as either garlic or onions. A seasonal treat, they're one of the first vegetables to emerge from Kingbird Farm's defrosting soil after a long winter. Ramps are popular in restaurant kitchens, so you may have to compete with local chefs for a bunch or two.

This recipe suggests using them in butter to slather on grilled bread as accompaniment to the farmhouse breakfast. There's a very short window of opportunity to buy ramps at the market; making ramp butter is the best way to extend the season. Note: Grill the ramps for a minute or two before pulsing for a smoky flavor.

1 pound unsalted butter, softened
½ pound Kingbird Farm ramps, minced
kosher salt
freshly ground black pepper

1. In the bowl of a food processor, cream butter until smooth.

2. Add minced ramps and pulse until fully incorporated. Season with salt and pepper to taste.

3. Set aside a small amount to use right away, and store the rest by transferring mixture to a sheet of parchment paper, rolled into a cylinder, twisting the ends and wrapping in foil. Chill until solid.

Sauteed Komatsuna with Bacon

MAKES 4 SERVINGS

Seeking affordable land within the market's thirty-mile radius requirement, Tim and Noelia Springston purchased a twenty-nine-acre former dairy farm just east of Elmira. Named Oxbow Farm for the meander of a creek on their land, the family began growing Asian greens, unique offerings intended to set them apart from most other market vendors.

Members since 2010, they continue to look for odd and interesting niche crops, including komatsuna, or Japanese mustard spinach, a leafy green that becomes the center of attraction in an easy-to-make stir-fry. Togarashi, Japanese powdered seasoning, adds intrigue, occupying much the same place as salt and pepper in the American kitchen. You'll find it at an Asian grocery store or the Asian section of local grocery markets.

1 tablespoon olive oil
½ medium Valley View Farm onion, chopped
2 cloves garlic, minced
1 bunch Oxbow Farm komatsuna, washed and sliced into 2-inch lengths
4 slices Cayuta Sun Farm bacon, cooked and chopped
½ teaspoon togarashi

1. Add oil to a large skillet or wok over medium heat. Add the onions and cook until translucent, about 5 minutes.

2. Add the garlic and cook for another minute.

3. Stir in komatsuna and cook until wilted and bright green. Remove from heat and stir in bacon.

4. Transfer to a warmed serving plate, season with togarashi, and pass family style around the table.

Skillet Broccolini

MAKES 4 SERVINGS

Mary McGarry-Newman of Buried Treasures Organic Farm explains that broccolini is not a young version of broccoli, but rather a cross between broccoli and Chinese kale. It's vibrant green in color, has small florets, long stalks, and a few small leaves—an entirely different plant than the broccoli you're used to at the grocery store. The tender shoots have a sweetness and tenderness that broccoli sometimes doesn't have. It's a quick-cooking vegetable that makes a delightful spring side dish.

12 ounces Buried Treasures Organic
   Farm broccolini
1 tablespoon olive oil
juice of 1 lemon
kosher salt
freshly ground black pepper

1. Trim the ends off broccolini, then cut in half lengthwise.

2. Heat a cast-iron skillet over medium-high heat. Add oil to the pan. Add broccolini and saute until tender, about 5 to 7 minutes. Remove from heat.

3. Transfer to a warmed serving dish. Coat with lemon juice, and season with salt and pepper to taste. Pass family style around the table.

Spring Carrots with Herb Dip

MAKES 6 SERVINGS

Ed and Donnette Baptist of Fort Baptist Farm, members of the market since 2018, steward ten acres of land along Coddington Road just outside Ithaca. They grow Mokum carrots, an heirloom variety named after the location of the Seed Savers Exchange in Amsterdam, and tastiest for fresh eating in spring. These are slender beauties, measuring no longer than your hand, harvested when mature enough to develop juicy, sweet flavors. Lovely when naked and raw; serve on a big plate alongside a bowl of creamy herb dip.

1 cup sour cream

1 cup mayonnaise

½ cup chopped parsley

3 tablespoons chopped chives

1 tablespoon white wine vinegar

1 clove garlic, minced

¼ teaspoon paprika

kosher salt

freshly ground black pepper

1 bunch Fort Baptist Farm spring carrots, washed, trimmed, but not peeled

1. In a bowl, combine sour cream, mayonnaise, parsley, chives, vinegar, garlic, and paprika. Season with salt and pepper, to taste. Mix well.

2. Cover and refrigerate until ready to use. Serve with spring carrots.

Stinging Nettles Soup

MAKES 4 SERVINGS

You might have encountered stinging nettles while hiking or running the trails around Ithaca. Brushing against this leafy green weed produces an intense burning sensation; the plant's stems and undersides of its leaves are irritating to human skin.

Harvested in early spring, nettles have a grassy, herbaceous, salty flavor, and in this dense, dark-green soup, you can almost taste the healthful bone-building minerals. Note: Be sure to wear gloves when handling fresh nettles.

1 pound Six Circles Farm stinging nettles
2 teaspoons salt
1 tablespoon olive oil
½ medium Valley View Farm Candy onion, diced
¼ cup basmati rice
4 cups chicken stock
sea salt
freshly ground black pepper

1. Bring a large pot of salted water to a boil. Drop in the nettles, blanching 1 to 2 minutes to remove most of the sting. Drain in a colander, and rinse with cold water. Trim stems, then chop coarsely.

2. Heat the olive oil in a saucepan over medium-low heat. Add the diced onions and cook about 5 minutes. Stir in the rice, chicken stock, and chopped nettles. Bring to a boil, then reduce heat to medium-low, cover, and simmer until the rice is tender, about 15 minutes.

3. Puree the soup with an immersion blender. Season with salt and pepper to taste.

4. To serve, ladle into each of 4 warmed bowls.

Sweet Maple Syrup Cornbread

MAKES 4 TO 6 SERVINGS

Donald and Daniel Weed of Schoolyard Sugarbush have been engaged in the annual ritual of "sugaring" for the production of fine maple syrup since the early 1990s. Maple sap collected from vigorous regional tree stands is boiled down in a flat, shallow steel pan called an evaporator. As it thickens, the syrup is drained off and filtered. Delicate flavors from the first sap flows during the sugaring season meet the springtime harvest of wildflower honey to provide a sweetness perfect for a moist and flavorful cornbread baked to a golden brown. Serve alongside a bowl of chili or stew.

olive oil
1 cup yellow cornmeal
1 cup all-purpose flour
1 tablespoon baking powder
1 teaspoon sea salt
¼ cup unsalted butter, melted and
 slightly cooled
¼ cup Waid's Apiaries wildflower
 honey
¼ cup Schoolyard Sugarbush maple
 syrup
2 Kingbird Farm chicken eggs, lightly
 beaten
1 cup Crosswinds Creamery milk

1. Preheat oven to 400 degrees F. Grease an 8-by-8-inch baking pan with the oil.

2. In a large bowl, sift together the cornmeal, flour, baking powder, and salt.

3. Make a well in the center of the dry ingredients and add the butter, honey, maple syrup, eggs, and milk. Stir to combine.

4. Pour batter into the prepared baking pan, spreading out evenly using a spatula.

5. Bake until browned on top and a toothpick or thin knife inserted in the top comes out clean, about 20 to 25 minutes. Remove from oven and allow to cool before serving.

Tatsoi and Daikon Radish Salad with Rhubarb Dressing

MAKES 4 SERVINGS

The high tunnels, or hoop houses, at Oxbow Farm are the covered structures that extend the growing season, protecting the tender Asian greens from unpredictable early spring weather.

Tatsoi is native to a region near the Yangtze River in central China. Over time, it was introduced into Korea and eventually brought to Japan, where it is considered essential to Japanese cuisine. With rounded leaves shaped like a spoon, tatsoi has a buttery texture and a slightly sweet, mustardy flavor. In this dish, the partnership of earthy tatsoi and crisp daikon radishes marries with sweet-tart rhubarb dressing.

1 bunch Oxbow Farm tatsoi leaves, washed and chopped
4 Stick and Stone daikon radishes, thinly sliced into sticks
rhubarb dressing*

1. Add tatsoi and radishes to a large bowl and toss.

2. Combine salad with dressing and toss to combine.

3. To serve, divide among 4 chilled salad plates.

*For the rhubarb dressing:

2 cups chopped Knapp Farm rhubarb
¼ cup sugar
¼ cup white vinegar
¾ cup extra-virgin olive oil
3 tablespoons grated Valley View Farm Candy onion
1 teaspoon Worcestershire sauce
½ teaspoon sea salt

1. Place rhubarb and ¼ cup water in a small saucepan. Bring to a boil over medium-high heat. Reduce heat and simmer 5 minutes until soft. Cool to room temperature.

2. Place in a blender or food processor with remaining ingredients and blend until smooth.

"Wide Awake" French Breakfast Radish Sandwiches

MAKES 4 SERVINGS

They are instantly recognizable at the West Haven Farm stand. French breakfast radishes are oblong rather than round or spherical, with a two-toned root, beginning as a beautiful pink at the top and transitioning into a milky white tip. Harvesting just after a frost brings out the sweetness in these little beauties. For this early spring sandwich, the mild, slightly sweet radishes partner with peppery, spicy arugula on a Wide Awake Bakery baguette.

Originating in France, breakfast radishes were first developed in 1879 and quickly became a favorite in Parisian markets, although the French didn't really eat them for breakfast. It was upper-class Victorians who were apparently fond of eating these mild little vegetables during the first meal of the day.

1 Wide Awake Bakery baguette

1½ sticks unsalted butter, room temperature

sea salt

2 bunches West Haven Farm French breakfast radishes, washed, trimmed, and thinly sliced

1 small handful arugula, trimmed

chives, chopped into chiffonade

1. Slice the baguette lengthwise and then crosswise, creating four quarters. Spread butter on the sliced side of each quarter and sprinkle with salt.

2. Pile sliced radishes onto the bottoms, then lay the arugula on top. Scatter with chives. Top the sandwiches and press down firmly. Serve immediately.

MAIN DISHES

Garlic Butter Chicken with Riesling

MAKES 4 SERVINGS

King Ferry Winery, the winegrowing endeavor begun by Peter and Taci Saltonstall, has become one of the true institutions of Finger Lakes wine country. As market vendors since 1991, the Saltonstalls offer a range of their estate-grown Treleaven wines, including exceptional Rieslings.

A good rule for cooking with wine: the wine should be good enough to sip while cooking. This dish of tender, juicy chicken is bathed in Treleaven semisweet Riesling, made in the style of a German Spätlese, and rich garlic butter sauce.

3 tablespoons extra-virgin olive oil
4 Just a Few Acres Farm boneless
   skinless chicken breasts
kosher salt
freshly ground black pepper
¾ cup Treleaven semisweet Riesling
4 tablespoons unsalted butter
1 tablespoon finely minced garlic
parsley, chopped into chiffonade

1. To a large skillet, heat the olive oil over medium-high heat. Evenly season the chicken with salt and pepper to taste, and cook until browned, about 5 to 6 minutes.

2. Turn the breasts and cook for another 5 to 6 minutes. Remove from skillet and set aside.

3. Deglaze skillet by adding wine and allowing the liquid to bubble up for a few seconds. Add the butter and allow it to melt, about 1 minute; stir until melted. Add the garlic and cook, about 1 minute.

4. To serve, place a chicken breast on each of 4 warmed dinner plates. Spoon sauce over each and garnish with parsley.

Pasta con Asparagi

MAKES 4 SERVINGS

Dennis and Marsha Bauchle of Straight-Way Farm have been tending the same patch of asparagus on their 150-acre farm in Schuyler County for fifteen years. After many years at Steamboat Landing, now you'll find them at the Wednesday Market on East Hill.

In Northern Italy, asparagus is an essential ingredient in the spring kitchen, not surprising, since the Veneto region grows the most asparagus in Italy. This recipe is a typical Venetian way of combining asparagus with pasta. Sweet, tender Purple Passion asparagus from Straight-Way Farm combines with linguine, or "little tongues" in Italian, which describes the long pasta noodles, in a dish that tastes like spring. Shop for asparagus with tightly closed tips and smooth, firm stalks.

6 fresh Straight-Way Farm Purple
    Passion asparagus spears
¾ pound dried linguine
2 tablespoons butter
sea salt
freshly ground black pepper
2 tablespoons basil, chopped into
    chiffonade
freshly grated Parmesan cheese

1. Bring a large pot of salted water to a boil.

2. Slice asparagus spears into 1-inch lengths, discarding tough ends.

3. Add asparagus to the boiling water and cook until just tender (thin spears take about 3 minutes, and thick spears take about 5 minutes). Remove asparagus with a slotted spoon and set aside.

4. Add linguine to the boiling pot. Cook to desired degree of doneness. Drain pasta, reserving 2 tablespoons cooking water.

5. Heat the butter in the pot. Add the asparagus and the linguini. Season with salt and pepper to taste. Add the reserved cooking water and basil. Toss to combine.

6. Remove from heat and divide among 4 warmed dinner plates. Serve with Parmesan on the side.

Slow-Poached Eggs

MAKES 4 SERVINGS

M. F. K. Fisher was the first to write about food as a way of understanding the world. She once wrote, "The finest way to know that the egg you plan to eat is a fresh one is to own the hen that makes the egg."

The next best way is to pick up a dozen eggs from Kingbird Farm, where in spring the flock of Rhode Island Red, Plymouth Blue Rock, and Australorp hens leaves the barn to forage across rich pastures and scratch up spent vegetable fields. In this dish, a Japanese cooking technique makes soft, creamy poached eggs that ooze perfectly over the Sunchoke and Bacon Breakfast Hash (see page 27).

4 Kingbird Farm chicken eggs

1. Fit a large pot with a steamer rack and fill with water. Place over low heat.

2. Clip a thermometer to the side of the pot and monitor the temperature. When the water reaches between 140 and 145 degrees F, add eggs to pot. Cook eggs for 30 to 35 minutes.

3. To serve, crack open eggs, one at a time, into small individual saucers.

Sunchoke and Bacon Breakfast Hash

MAKES 4 SERVINGS

If you visit the Kingbird Farm stand at the market, perhaps you'll come across these odd, knobby vegetables that slightly resemble ginger. Sunchokes are grown on the small, family-owned organic farm in Berkshire, run by Michael, Karma, and Rosemary Glos. Harvested in early spring, sunchokes have an earthy, nutty flavor that some compare to a potato, and in this recipe, sunchokes take on the role of a potato with local pig-belly bacon, scallions, and arugula to create a market-inspired breakfast dish.

1 pound Kingbird Farm sunchokes, unpeeled, cut into ½-inch-thick slices
4 teaspoons extra-virgin olive oil, divided
6 ounces uncooked Cayuta Sun Farm bacon, diced
½ cup scallions, chopped
1 cup arugula, roughly chopped
1 tablespoon minced garlic
kosher salt
freshly ground black pepper

1. Place sunchokes in a medium saucepan, add enough water to cover, and bring to a boil over high heat. Reduce heat to medium-low and simmer, covered, until sunchokes are tender, about 8 to 10 minutes. Remove from heat and drain.

2. Heat two teaspoons of oil in a large skillet over medium-high heat. Add bacon and scallions. Cook, stirring until bacon begins to brown, about 5 minutes. Add remaining oil, arugula, garlic, salt, pepper, and sunchokes.

3. Cook, stirring the mix until the sunchokes are lightly mashed, about 4 to 5 minutes. Remove from heat.

4. To serve, divide hash among four warmed dinner plates. Top each serving with a Slow-Poached Egg (see page 26).

Vino Bianco–Baked Salmon with Fresh Dill

MAKES 4 SERVINGS

The word dill is derived from the Norse word dilla, meaning to lull, to sing a lullaby, to soothe young children, and later used to describe the soothing and calming effect of dill. The feathery fresh herb adds warm, complex flavors of caraway and fennel to this preparation of wild-caught salmon.

For the wine, visit the Damiani Wine Cellars stand and pick up a bottle of Vino Bianco. It's a vibrant blend of Grüner Veltliner, Riesling, and sauvignon blanc, grown on vineyards in the subclimate known as the Banana Belt on the eastern side of Seneca Lake.

4 wild-caught salmon fillets
1 tablespoon olive oil
sea salt
freshly ground black pepper
1 lemon, sliced
6 sprigs of fresh dill, plus more for
   serving, chopped
½ cup Damiani Wine Cellars Vino
   Blanco

1. Preheat oven to 325 degrees F.

2. Lightly oil and season both sides of the salmon with salt and pepper. Arrange lemon slices and dill on the bottom of a baking dish, and place the salmon fillets, skin-side down, onto the bed of lemon and dill.

3. Pour wine into the baking dish. Cover with aluminum foil. Bake salmon fillets, about 12 to 18 minutes, depending on thickness (thickest part of each fillet should reach 125 degrees F).

4. To serve, transfer a salmon fillet to each of 4 warmed dinner plates. Garnish each with chopped dill.

DESSERT

"Victoria" Rhubarb Sorbet

MAKES 1 QUART

Knapp Farm was founded in 1796 by Jacob Lowman, who purchased the land from Captain John Spaulding, a Revolutionary War soldier and veteran of the Sullivan Campaign. Fully half of the farm is situated on the site of the Battle of Newtown, fought during the Revolutionary War.

Those vibrant ruby-colored stalks at the Knapp Farm stand are a telltale sign of spring. Ellen Knapp arrives with Victoria rhubarb, an heirloom variety first bred more than one hundred years ago in England and named in honor of Queen Victoria by its creator, Joseph Myatt. Its bright, tart flavor is tamed with sugar in this refreshing, pink-hued, early spring treat.

1 pound Knapp Farm rhubarb, chopped
1 cup caster sugar
¼ teaspoon sea salt
2 tablespoons fresh lime juice
1 cup water

1. Combine rhubarb, sugar, salt, lime juice, and water in a skillet and simmer over medium heat for 8 to 10 minutes, until softened.

2. Puree rhubarb mixture in a blender until smooth, about 2 minutes. Allow to cool.

3. Pour the puree into an ice cream maker and churn according to the manufacturer's directions.

4. Transfer to an airtight container and store in the freezer until sorbet is firm, about 1 hour.

ITHACA FARMERS MARKET HISTORY: 1973

The year was 1973. The United States signed a peace accord and withdrew troops from Vietnam, ending twelve years of combat in Southeast Asia. The Supreme Court ruled on *Roe v. Wade*, legalizing abortion. In pop culture, the Beatles had disbanded, as Led Zeppelin, Pink Floyd, and the Who emerged

In Crust We Trust, Everhart Bread, 1975

on the music scene. The year's most popular films were *The Exorcist* and *American Graffiti*. Back-to-the-land and environmental movements began to explore ecologically focused ideas around farming and selling agricultural products directly to consumers at common, recurrent physical locations. A group of local activists formed the Ithaca Real Food Co-op (now Greenstar), owned by the people who shopped there.

It was in the spring of that year when Ann Rider and neighbor David Rindos met on Ann's porch to discuss the idea of a local farmers market in Ithaca. Ann, who grew up on her family's sixty-acre farm on Sirrine Road in Trumansburg, was a baker and caterer, looking for new ways to sell her breads and pastries. David was a Cornell-trained archaeologist who would later write an important book on the origins of agriculture and had visited the Portland, Oregon, farmers market, established a year earlier.

David suggested a similar market in Ithaca, one that would support local food growers and producers and create a place for vibrant community

High Fashion at Jan Norman's Silk Oak, 1980

gatherings. He thought that every item offered for sale should be grown, produced, or crafted within a strict thirty-mile radius of the city. Ann wanted 60 percent of the vendors to be local farmers selling farm goods with the other 40 percent split between craft vendors and food vendors.

The enterprise they envisioned began modestly. On Saturday, August 18, 1973, a small contingent of agrarians and craftspeople pulled their trucks and station wagons onto an empty lot at Fulton Street near the Agway farm store. Some displayed goods on the tailgates of vehicles, others under a patchwork of canvas tents and makeshift tables.

Locals arrived by car, on bicycle, or on foot from surrounding neighborhoods. Sellers, many of whom had been unable to gain access to conventional markets, used handwritten cardboard signs to identify fresh-picked vegetables and fruits, baked items, and crafts. The turnout was encouraging, and vendors continued to meet on successive Saturdays through the end of the season.

Music Man Dave Davies (on trombone) and Friends, 1995

The Early Years, Inlet Island, 1975

A second location on the old airport runway near the Hangar Theater was outgrown by 1975, and the expanding colony of vendors resettled on an expanse of empty land along Inlet Island. Railroad tracks leading to the coal-fired plant across the lake passed nearby, and on market days the whistle of freight trains was often heard harmonizing with live bluegrass music.

As the market continued to expand, traffic and parking overflowed, and it was time for another move, this time to an empty lot downtown, where the forces of urban renewal had removed an ancient department store.

"Never doubt that a small group of thoughtful, committed citizens can change the world," writes Margaret Mead. "Indeed, it is the only thing that ever has."

SUMMER

Summer cooking implies a sense of immediacy, a capacity to capture the essence of the fleeting moment.

—Elizabeth David

BEVERAGES AND COCKTAILS

Haymaker's Punch

MAKES 4 DRINKS

Generations ago, thirsty farmers prepared this drink to help rehydrate and reenergize during the summer hay harvest. Sweet and sour, with the spicy edge of ginger, the market-inspired Haymaker's Punch is guaranteed to refresh, replenish lost electrolytes, and provide a boost of energy during midseason in Ithaca.

Berkshire Hills wildflower honey comes from families of hives in pristine areas along the high hills of Berkshire in Tioga County. It is a pure harvested honey that does not undergo any type of heat or physical treatment to preserve freshness and genuineness.

8 cups water, room temperature

¼ cup Littletree Orchards apple cider vinegar

2 teaspoons freshly grated Humble Hill Farm baby ginger

¼ cup + 2 tablespoons Berkshire Hills Honey Bee Farm wildflower honey

¼ teaspoon sea salt

1. Add water to a half-gallon jar with a lid.

2. Stir vinegar, ginger, honey, and sea salt into the water. Top the jar with lid, place in the fridge, and chill overnight.

3. To serve, strain into 4 tall glasses filled with ice.

Il Pomodoro

MAKES 1 DRINK

Italians are deeply versed in gioie della tavola, *the moments of pure joy that take place around the table. They understand and appreciate the synergy created when conversation and laughter commingle with the pleasure of savoring food and drink. In this decidedly Italian approach to the Bloody Mary, fresh, fragrant basil and rich, ripe tomatoes complement one another in a market-inspired cocktail, animated with the blithe sparkle of prosecco. Cool and restrained, Il Pomodoro is designed to be paired with a warm-weather dinner.*

1 ounce vodka, chilled
3 Jackman Vineyards cherry tomatoes
pinch of sea salt
prosecco, chilled
2 fresh basil sprigs

1. Add the vodka to a highball glass filled with ice.

2. Squeeze cherry tomatoes over the ice, then drop them in.

3. Add pinch of salt, top up with prosecco, and tuck basil sprigs into the glass.

The Lucky Jim

In Kingsley Amis's On Drink (1970), the grand old man of English letters devised this derivative of the vodka martini. "What you serve should be treated with respect," he writes, "not because it is specially strong but because it tastes specially mild and bland." For visual decor, he suggests leaving the peel on the floating cucumber slice. His first novel, Lucky Jim (1954), is regarded by many as the finest—and funniest—comic novel of the twentieth century.

As for cocktail hour, something magical happens when the basic ingredients are shaken with cucumber juice and strained into a martini glass—the drink cleanses, refreshes, and energizes the palate before dinner.

2½ ounces vodka, chilled
¼ ounce French vermouth
¼ ounce cucumber juice*
cucumber slice

1. Combine liquid ingredients in a mixing glass filled with cracked ice.

2. Shake vigorously and strain into a chilled martini glass. Float cucumber slice on top.

*For the cucumber juice:

1 Humble Hill Farm Silver Slicer cucumber, peeled and cut
   into 1-inch sections
squeezed juice of ½ lemon
¼ cup water

1. Combine cucumber, lemon juice, and water in a blender and blend. Strain and discard the pulp.

Staycation

MAKES 1 DRINK

Blueberries have deep roots in Finger Lakes agricultural history, some that go back to the Native American tribes who first inhabited the region. They used the precious berries in many ways—as food, as medicine, and even as a dye for clothing.

Waiter, there's a blueberry in my drink! A crisp and refreshing summer sipper from the blend of vodka, fresh mint, a French aperitif, and plump blueberries from John Tamburello's farm in Trumansburg. A brilliant berry-colored drink, perfect for a midsummer night's cocktail party.

8 to 10 Glenhaven Farm blueberries
sprig of fresh mint
1½ ounces vodka
½ ounce Lillet Blanc
½ ounce fresh lime juice
½ ounce simple syrup
3 dashes mint bitters (optional)

1. Muddle blueberries and mint sprig in a mixing glass.

2. Add remaining ingredients in the mixing glass and fill with cracked ice.

3. Shake vigorously and strain into a rocks glass over new ice.

Strawberry Milkshakes with Basil Whipped Cream

MAKES 2 DRINKS

"The cow is of the bovine ilk," quips Ogden Nash, "One end is moo, the other milk."

Happy, healthy Brown Swiss cows graze smack-dab on lush acres of rolling green pastureland at Crosswinds Farm in Rock Stream. From May through October or November, they feast on dry hay or baleage through the winter. And—holy cow!—on average, they produce about forty pounds of milk per day.

There's nothing more fitting on a midsummer day in Ithaca than a soda fountain-inspired mix of strawberries and cream, fresh-picked West Haven Farm strawberries, creamy Crosswinds milk, and homemade ice cream.

Deliciously sweet, fragrant, and colorful, fresh strawberries are a feast for the senses. The arrival of Jewel strawberries, developed by Cornell AgriTech and grown on West Haven Farm, is one of the first signs of summer.

½ pound West Haven Farm Jewel strawberries, hulled and sliced
2 tablespoons sugar
1 teaspoon vanilla extract
1 pint vanilla ice cream (see Chester Platt's Cherry "Sunday," page 77)
½ cup Crosswinds Creamery milk
basil whipped cream*

1. In a mixing bowl, combine the sliced strawberries, sugar, and vanilla extract, and stir well to combine. Set aside and allow to macerate for at least 20 minutes and up to 1 hour.

2. In a large blender, place the strawberry mixture, ice cream, and milk. Blend until smooth. Pour into 2 tall glasses.

*For the basil whipped cream:

1 cup heavy cream
handful of fresh basil, torn into pieces
2½ tablespoons sugar

1. Combine cream and basil in a small saucepan. Cover and heat over medium heat, until small bubbles begin to form on the surface. Remove from heat and refrigerate until cold, allowing basil to steep in cream.

2. Pour the cream into a small bowl through a mesh strainer to remove the basil.

3. Transfer cold cream mixture to the bowl of a stand mixer fitted with a whisk attachment (or use a hand mixer). Beat on high and slowly stream in sugar until the cream holds its shape.

SALADS AND SMALL PLATES

"Abundance" Salt Potatoes

MAKES 6 SERVINGS

Among the display of potatoes at the Sabol's Farm stand, you'll find a golf ball–sized variety called "Abundance," named for its consistently high yield. Since this variety was developed by the Cornell breeding program, these creamy, nutty, and buttery (even without butter) potatoes are perfect partners with Dr. Baker's Cornell Barbecue Chicken (see page 68).

The salt potato preparation is a regional tradition invented by Syracuse salt mine workers who created a simple and inexpensive lunch by boiling small potatoes in local brine.

2 quarts water
1 pound kosher salt
2 pounds Sabol's Farm Abundance
   potatoes
¾ stick butter
parsley, chopped into chiffonade

1. Wash the potatoes thoroughly. Cut out any bad spots or growing eyes, but leave the skin on and the potatoes whole.

2. Bring the water to a hard boil. Add the salt and stir until dissolved. Add the potatoes. Boil until a fork slides in and out of a potato with ease, about 20 to 25 minutes.

3. Drain the potatoes in a strainer or colander. Let sit for a few minutes and they should develop a slight frosting of salt. Return the hot pot to the burner and turn it to medium. Add the butter and melt. Add potatoes and stir to coat with butter.

4. Transfer to a large serving bowl, scatter parsley over the top, and pass family style around the table.

Blistered Shishito Peppers

MAKES 4 APPETIZER SERVINGS

Shishito means "lion," a reference to the cap of the Japanese heirloom pepper, which resembles a lion's mane. Blistered shishito peppers are popular bar bites served in Japanese izakayas, informal after-work bars. Charred and blistered, the grassy-flavored, slightly smoky peppers partner perfectly with a pint of ice-cold beer.

4 heaping cups Oxbow Farm shishito peppers
1 to 2 tablespoons extra-virgin olive oil
2 teaspoons fresh lemon juice
Maldon sea salt flakes

1. Rinse peppers and pat dry. Heat olive oil over medium-high heat in a cast-iron skillet. When the pan is hot, add the peppers in a single layer and cook until blistered, about 3 to 4 minutes. Flip and cook until blistered and tender, another 1 to 2 minutes.

2. Transfer to a bowl and toss with lemon juice.

3. On a serving platter, arrange peppers around a small bowl of salt flakes.

Bloody Mary Tomato Salad

MAKES 4 SERVINGS

Perhaps the finest and most persistent version of the morning palliative, the Bloody Mary was popularized after the repeal of Prohibition by barman Fernand Petiot at the iconic King Cole Bar in New York's St. Regis Hotel to help ease sufferers into the day. Beyond treatment for a hangover, the basic elements of the classic cocktail become inspiration for a simple summer tomato salad. Skip the vodka, of course.

Doug Newman and Mary McGarry-Newman of Buried Treasures Organic Farm grow six hundred to seven hundred tomato plants, mostly heirlooms, in four high tunnels to keep them safe from extreme weather and away from notorious tomato bandits (raccoons, squirrels, and chipmunks). Doug says choosing a favorite tomato for a sandwich is like choosing his favorite child, so he recommends picking up an "heirloom sampler" for as wide an array of options as possible.

2 pounds Buried Treasures Organic
 Farm mixed heirloom tomatoes
kosher salt
freshly ground black pepper
squeezed juice of ½ lemon
2 teaspoons Tabasco
3 tablespoons extra-virgin olive oil
celery seeds
parsley, chopped into chiffonade

1. Using a serrated knife, cut a thin slice from the top and bottom of each tomato then cut each tomato in half. Cut halves into slices ⅜- to ¼-inch thick.

2. Assemble by overlapping tomato slices on a serving platter and season generously with salt and pepper.

3. Add lemon juice, Tabasco, and olive oil to a small bowl and whisk to combine. Drizzle dressing over the tomatoes.

4. Sprinkle with celery seeds and parsley. Pass family style around the table.

Cherry Tomato Confit

MAKES 4 TO 6 SERVINGS

A wise newspaperman by the name of Lewis Grizzard once wrote, "It's difficult to think of anything but pleasant thoughts while eating homegrown tomatoes."

Slow-roasted, tangy-sweet tomatoes in olive oil, with the aromatics of garlic and fresh thyme, make a versatile condiment. Serve over thick slices of grilled bread, toss with pasta, spoon over cooked chicken or fish, add to a cheese plate . . .

2 pints Jackman Farm Sungold mixed cherry tomatoes, stemmed
4 Six Circles Farm Spanish Roja garlic cloves, smashed
1 cup extra-virgin olive oil
4 fresh thyme sprigs
1 teaspoon kosher salt

1. Preheat oven to 275 degrees F.

2. In a baking dish, place tomatoes and garlic in a single layer. Pour olive oil over the tomatoes and add thyme and salt.

3. Cover tightly with aluminum foil and bake, about 1½ to 2 hours, or until the oil is hot but the tomatoes remain whole.

4. Let tomato mixture cool to room temperature. Store with accumulated juices in an airtight container until ready to use.

Chow-Chow for Hot Dogs

MAKES 6 TO 8 SERVINGS

Grilled hot dogs are an American backyard summer tradition, and a hot dog can become an entire meal with this market-inspired topping. Chow-Chow gives the dog a personality. The beauty of this southern-inspired slaw is that you can make it different every time, adding other vegetables, including red or green tomatoes, carrots, beans, or peas. If this sounds messy, be assured that, architecturally speaking, the worst that can happen is that a little bit falls into your lap.

1½ cups Littletree Orchards apple
  cider vinegar
1 cup sugar
2 teaspoons celery seeds
2 teaspoons mustard seeds
2 teaspoons dry mustard
1 teaspoon turmeric
1 tablespoon salt
1 small head Nook & Cranny Farm
  Storage #4 cabbage, shredded
1 medium Valley View Farm Candy
  onion, finely chopped
1 Jackman Vineyards Italian sweet
  pepper, chopped
2 tablespoons extra-virgin olive oil

1. In a medium saucepan, bring the cider vinegar, sugar, celery seeds, mustard seeds, dry mustard, turmeric, and salt to a boil.

2. Add the cabbage, chopped onions, and peppers to the boiling mixture. Simmer for about 10 minutes. Remove from heat.

3. Transfer the mixture into a large bowl, and toss with the olive oil. Cover and refrigerate until ready to serve.

Corn on the Cob with Parsley-Garlic Butter

MAKES 4 SERVINGS

In Walden, *published in 1854 and based on his life at Walden Pond, Henry David Thoreau asks, "Pray what more can a reasonable man desire, in peaceful times, in ordinary noons, than a sufficient number of ears of green sweet-corn boiled, with the addition of salt?"*

Few things symbolize the peak of summer more than a crop of sweet corn picked early in the morning and offered that same day at the market. Corn on the cob may be the most anticipated, most revered vegetable grown in our region. Since 1994, Mandeville Farm in rural Spencer has provided picnics, clambakes, barbecues, and backyard summer suppers with an early season variety called Kickoff, the sweetest, juiciest, most flavorful corn you ever put in your mouth.

1 stick unsalted butter, softened
1 cup parsley, finely chopped
1 Six Circles Farm Spanish Roja garlic
  clove, minced
4 ears Mandeville Farm Kickoff corn,
  husks and silk removed
kosher salt
freshly ground black pepper

1. In a food processor, pulse the butter with the parsley and garlic to combine; scrape down the bowl as needed. Transfer the parsley-garlic butter to a small bowl and set aside.

2. Bring a large pot of salted water to a boil and add the corn. Cook until the corn is tender and bright yellow, about 2 to 3 minutes. Using tongs, place corn on a rack and cool slightly.

3. Transfer corn to a serving platter. Generously brush each ear of corn with the parsley-garlic butter. Season with salt and pepper to taste.

Cucumber Picnic Salad

MAKES 4 SERVINGS

Most cucumbers are modest. Not the Silver Slicers. From mid-July to late summer, look for this variety, fresh off the vine, at the Humble Hill Farm stand. They have a creamy white, thin skin and a juicy, sweet crunch. The best ones are on the smaller side before seeds develop and the flesh gets watery.

Basil-infused vinegar, sugar, salt, and onion add zest to every bite of this salad. Use a mandoline slicer for evenly sliced cucumbers. Marinating the prepared salad for an hour or so softens the bite of the onions and allows the seasonings to infuse.

1 pound Humble Hill Farm Silver Slicer cucumbers, thinly sliced
1½ teaspoons sugar
1 teaspoon kosher salt
2½ tablespoons Littletree Orchards basil-infused apple cider vinegar
½ medium Valley View Farm Candy onion, thinly sliced

1. In a medium bowl, toss cucumber slices with the sugar and salt. Stir in the vinegar and onion and refrigerate for at least 1 hour.

2. Transfer into a covered container for transport to the picnic.

Garlic Scape Chimichurri

MAKES 8 TO 10 SERVINGS

The long, leafless flower stalks that fall-planted garlic sends up in late spring and early summer are one of the best-kept secrets of the market. This version of chimichurri, a traditional Argentine pesto, is composed of fresh parsley, oregano, shallot, oil, and vinegar, complementing the vibrant green stalks of organically grown garlic scapes from Six Circles Farm, located on the eastern shore of Seneca Lake in Lodi.

In Argentina, chimichurri is traditionally served with grilled steak, but the tangy, herbaceous sauce also elevates chicken, fish, or pasta dishes, and it's great just slathered on crusty bread. For chunky texture, hand-chop the ingredients rather than using a blender or food processor.

½ pound Six Circles Farm garlic scapes, finely chopped

¼ cup fresh oregano leaves, finely chopped

¼ cup flat leaf parsley, finely chopped

1 medium shallot, finely chopped

¼ cup red wine vinegar

½ cup extra-virgin olive oil

½ teaspoon sea salt

⅛ teaspoon freshly ground black pepper

¼ teaspoon red pepper flakes

1. Combine all ingredients in a large bowl or container and mix thoroughly.

2. Cover and refrigerate until ready to serve.

Heirloom Tomato Pico de Gallo

MAKES 4 TO 6 SERVINGS

Journalist Raymond Sokolov explains, "Real (as I will call vine-ripened, soft-walled, acid-flavored, Summer-grown) tomatoes are an article of faith, a rallying point for the morally serious, a grail."

Tomato varieties grown for at least fifty years without cross-breeding are called heirlooms. These richly flavored beauties are the stars of the summer market. You can tell a farmer's passions by the tomatoes she grows. Cherokee Purple, Brandywine, Black Krim, and Striped German are a few of the colorful heirlooms grown at Stick and Stone Farm. If you ask Lucy Garrison-Clauson which one tastes best, she'll tell you that she only grows the ones she likes.

Pico de gallo, or salsa fresca, is always best in the middle of tomato season, made with the most flavorful heirloom tomatoes you can find. Serve as a dip with tortilla chips.

½ medium Valley View Farm Candy onion, chopped

1 medium Jackman Vineyards jalapeño or serrano pepper, ribs and seeds removed and finely chopped

¼ cup lime juice

1 teaspoon sea salt

4 Stick and Stone Farm heirloom tomatoes, chopped

½ cup cilantro, chopped into chiffonade

1. In a medium mixing bowl, combine the chopped onion, jalapeño, lime juice, and salt. Allow it marinate for about 5 minutes while you chop the tomatoes and cilantro.

2. Add the chopped tomatoes and cilantro to the bowl and stir to combine. Allow mixture to marinate at least 1 hour in the refrigerator.

3. Transfer to a chilled bowl. Serve with tortilla chips.

"June Kale" Caesar Salad with Garlic Croutons

MAKES 4 SERVINGS

Chaw Chang and Lucy Garrison-Clauson raise forty to fifty acres of certified organic vegetables each year at Stick and Stone Farm, just a few miles northwest of Ithaca. They've been stalwart members of the market since 1996. "Organic kale is available almost every month of the year," explains Lucy, "although it changes character, from tender, first-picking June kale to spicy late-summer kale, to hearty, stew-worthy fall kale, and early winter kale from the field, transitioning to sweet tender high-tunnel kale in the heart of winter, then spunky kale raab in spring."

4 cups chopped Stick and Stone Farm curly kale
1 recipe Caesar dressing*
2 cups garlic croutons**

1. When ready to serve, add kale and croutons to a large serving bowl with the dressing; toss until well coated. Divide among 4 chilled salad plates.

*For the Caesar dressing:

3 anchovy fillets, drained
2 Six Circles Farm Spanish Roja garlic cloves
2 Jasper Meadows Farm duck egg yolks
⅓ cup freshly grated Parmesan
2 tablespoons fresh lemon juice
1 teaspoon Dijon mustard
¼ teaspoon sea salt
pinch of freshly ground black pepper
½ cup extra-virgin olive oil

1. Add anchovy fillets, garlic, egg yolks, Parmesan, lemon juice, mustard, salt, and pepper to a blender. Puree until combined.

2. While the blender is running, gradually stream in the olive oil until the dressing is completely smooth.

(continued)

**For the garlic croutons:

2 tablespoons unsalted butter

2 tablespoons extra-virgin olive oil

2 medium Six Circles Farm Spanish Roja garlic cloves,
  pressed

1 tablespoon fresh parsley, finely chopped

¼ teaspoon sea salt

¼ teaspoon freshly ground black pepper

½ loaf Wide Awake Bakery sourdough bread, cut into
  ¾-inch cubes

1. Preheat oven to 375 degrees F.

2. In a small saucepan, combine butter, olive oil, garlic cloves, chopped parsley, salt, and pepper. Heat over medium heat until butter is melted. Stir to combine then set aside.

3. Cut bread into ¾-inch cubes. Transfer to a large mixing bowl.

4. Drizzle the seasoned olive oil over the chopped bread and toss until the bread has an even coating of oil.

5. Bake until golden, 15 to 20 minutes, turning once halfway through cooking to brown all sides.

Massaged Kale Salad with Balsamic Blueberry Vinaigrette

MAKES 4 SERVINGS

Raw kale is fibrous and chewy compared to other greens, so it requires a bit of massage therapy. Working kale leaves with your hands tames the texture and renders them tender enough to eat without cooking. A splash of olive oil and citrus helps break down the cell walls in the curly leaves, relaxing and tenderizing them, and salt combined with the warmth of your hands draws out the moisture in the leaves.

This salad is simple to prepare, and it can be doubled for a dinner party or halved for a light meal for one and served along with just about anything—chicken, steak, fish.

3 tablespoons extra-virgin olive oil
2 cloves Six Circles Farm Spanish Roja
   garlic, minced
1 bunch Stick and Stone Farm curly
   kale, stems removed
squeezed juice of 1 lemon
kosher salt
balsamic blueberry vinaigrette*

1. In a small skillet, heat the olive oil and minced garlic over medium heat for 30 seconds. Set the garlic-infused oil aside to cool.

2. Place the kale in a large bowl and toss in the cooled olive oil and lemon juice. Use clean hands to massage the kale, rubbing leaves together between your fingers, about 3 minutes, to tenderize and infuse the leaves with the oil and lemon. Add a pinch of salt near the end of massaging.

3. Toss the massaged kale with enough vinaigrette to coat. Arrange in separate piles on each of 4 chilled serving plates. Serve at once, passing extra vinaigrette around.

*For the balsamic blueberry vinaigrette:

1 cup fresh Glenhaven Farm blueberries
¼ cup balsamic vinegar
2 tablespoons Waid's Apiaries wildflower honey
1 tablespoon fresh lemon juice
sea salt
freshly cracked black pepper
½ cup extra-virgin olive oil

1. In a blender, combine blueberries, vinegar, honey, lemon juice, salt, and pepper.

2. With the blender running, slowly pour in olive oil. Continue blending until completely emulsified and creamy, about 30 seconds.

Mexican Street Corn Salad with Feta

MAKES 6 SERVINGS

Inspired by street food with roots in Mexico City, fresh-picked corn from Mandeville Farm serves as the primary ingredient in the salad version of elotes. Unlike the traditional antojito (little cravings), this recipe doesn't require a grill and instead chars the corn kernels in a hot skillet until browned and caramelized. Snow Farm Creamery feta cheese adds a salty, milky accent, and ancho chile powder adds smoky notes.

2 tablespoons olive oil

4 ears Mandeville Farm Kickoff corn, husks and silk removed, kernels cut from the cob

kosher salt

freshly ground black pepper

½ cup scallions, finely sliced

½ cup cilantro leaves, finely chopped

½ Jackman Vineyards jalapeño pepper, seeded and stemmed, finely chopped

2 cloves Six Circles Farm Spanish Roja garlic, minced

2 tablespoons mayonnaise

freshly squeezed juice from 1 lime

2 ounces Snow Farm Creamery feta cheese, finely crumbled

ancho chile powder

1. Heat oil in a cast-iron or heavy skillet over medium-high heat. Add corn kernels, season with salt and pepper, toss once or twice, and cook, stirring occasionally, until corn is charred, about 8 to 10 minutes.

2. In a large bowl, add scallions, cilantro, jalapeño, garlic, mayonnaise, and lime juice, and toss to combine.

3. Add charred corn to the bowl and toss to coat.

4. Transfer to a warmed serving platter. Spread the corn mixture in an even layer and scatter cheese and ancho chile powder over the top. Pass family style around the table.

Mixed Edible Flower Mignonette

MAKES 1 CUP

"That marvel of delicacy," writes Henry Ward Beecher, "that concentration of sapid excellence, that mouthful before all mouthfuls." To a purist, anything that adorns a raw oyster is unloved, but for the less devout, this simple recipe provides a garden-inspired mignonette sauce for oysters, clams, or other seafood, a lovely accompaniment to any briny dish.

Choose among bouquets of edible flowers at the Dirtbaby Farm stand, freshly picked from Kourtney Selak's garden on a small patch of land in Hector. Kourtney might suggest pansies, calendula, and cornflowers for their color and beauty and chive blossoms or nasturtiums for their spicy, flavorful kick. The mignonette can be served in a small bowl with a small spoon, alongside oysters on a platter (in French, plateau de coquillages).

⅓ cup coarsely chopped Dirtbaby Farm mixed edible flowers
⅓ cup finely minced shallots
⅓ cup white wine vinegar

1. Combine the chopped flowers with the shallots and vinegar.
2. Spoon 1 teaspoon of the mixture over each oyster.

Rainbow Carrots with Apple Cider Vinegar

MAKES 4 TO 6 SERVINGS

Members of the market since 1999, Rick Tarantelli and Courtney Sullivan are small-scale growers on a home-stead farm in Spencer. Overflowing, gorgeously colorful baskets of rainbow carrots entice marketgoers to the Humble Hill Farm stand.

Rick and Courtney grow rows of each color, then bundle them into a rainbow array. They vary in eye-candy colors, from purple to yellow to bright orange, and each color tastes subtly different. Purple carrots are spicy, mildly peppery, and high in anthocyanin, the same antioxidant in blueberries and elderberries; yellow carrots have an earthy flavor with notes of celery or parsley; beta-carotene-rich orange carrots are sweet and palate pleasing. In this dish, the carrots are brightened with lemon and apple cider vinegar.

12 Humble Hill Farm rainbow carrots

3 tablespoons extra-virgin olive oil

1½ teaspoons thyme leaves, minced

1 teaspoon kosher salt

½ teaspoon freshly ground black pepper

2 tablespoons fresh lemon juice

1 tablespoon Littletree Orchards apple cider vinegar

1. Preheat the broiler.

2. Cut the carrots crosswise into 4-inch lengths, then lengthwise into sticks.

3. Place the carrots on a sheet pan, drizzle with olive oil, and sprinkle with thyme, kosher salt, and pepper. Toss by hand to coat, then spread the carrots in an even layer.

4. Broil carrots, about 8 to 10 minutes, tossing every few minutes, until they are tender and slightly charred. Top with the lemon juice and apple cider vinegar, tossing to coat.

5. Transfer to a warmed serving bowl and pass family style around the table.

Sauteed Okra and Chile ·

MAKES 4 SERVINGS

Okra, also known as ladies' fingers, is tenacious and especially loves the midsummer heat. One hundred okra plants are grown on Jasper Meadows Farm in Freeville, harvested for delivery to the market beginning in late July. It's said the okra plant never grows taller than its planter.

Warm-season okra has a sweet, grassy flavor that takes on more depth with longer cooking. Red pepper flakes add another dimension of flavor to the dish without making every mouthful hot and spicy.

1 pound Jasper Meadows Farm okra
2 tablespoons extra-virgin olive oil
1 teaspoon crushed red pepper flakes
kosher salt
freshly ground black pepper

1. Rinse okra and pat dry. Using a sharp paring knife, cut off the tough stems.

2. Pour the oil into a large skillet over medium-high heat. Add the okra and red pepper flakes. Saute until okra has softened slightly but is still crisp, about 6 to 8 minutes. Season with salt and pepper to taste.

3. Transfer to a warmed serving dish and pass family style around the table.

"Scarborough Fair" Roasted Carrots

MAKES 4 SERVINGS

Parsley, sage, rosemary, and thyme are said to represent bitterness, strength, faithfulness, and courage. In 1966, the musical duo of Simon and Garfunkel covered an old English ballad called "Scarborough Fair," whose lyrics mention the four spices. The song entered popular culture when it was included on the soundtrack of The Graduate, *Mike Nichols's 1967 romantic comedy.*

Roasting carrots is the best way to bring out their inner natures. For this dish, summer-harvested Romance carrots from Shagbark Gardens are roasted in a high-temperature oven, creating caramelized edges and tender-crisp texture.

8 Shagbark Gardens Romance carrots, washed and peeled
2 tablespoons extra virgin olive oil
½ teaspoon kosher salt
¼ teaspoon freshly ground black pepper
2 teaspoons Scarborough Fair herb blend*

1. Preheat oven to 425 degrees F. Line a baking sheet with aluminum foil.

2. Slice the carrots on the diagonal, about 2 inches thick.

3. On the prepared baking sheet, toss together the carrots, olive oil, salt, pepper, and herb blend. Roast, stirring midway through cooking, until caramelized and tender, about 20 to 25 minutes (cooking time will depend on thickness of carrots). Remove from oven.

4. Transfer to a warmed serving bowl and pass family style around the table.

*For the Scarborough Fair herb blend:

1 tablespoon chopped fresh sage
1 tablespoon chopped fresh rosemary
1 tablespoon chopped fresh thyme
½ cup parsley, chopped into chiffonade

1. Place all herbs in a big bowl and use your hands to gently mix them together thoroughly.

Spinach Salad Balsamico

MAKES 4 SERVINGS

A favorite variety at Nook & Cranny Farm, Space is a medium-green, smooth-leaved spinach variety that maintains excellent flavor in a wide range of preparations. It's called "Space" because of its high yield, long harvest window, and exceptional field-holding quality.

Intensely flavored balsamic vinegars are made from reduced grape must aged for several years in wooden barrels, produced in either the province of Modena or Reggio Emilia, Italy. Carefully drizzle a small amount of vinaigrette over the spinach to start. You can always add more later to suit your taste.

4–6 cups Nook & Cranny Farm Space spinach
¾ cup extra-virgin olive oil
¼ cup balsamic vinegar
sea salt
freshly ground black pepper

1. Rinse the spinach in cold water. Spin it dry in a salad spinner and place in a large bowl.

2. In a jam jar or other container with a tight-fitting lid, combine olive oil and balsamic vinegar. Add a generous pinch of salt and a few grinds of black pepper. Tighten the lid and shake vigorously.

3. Sprinkle the spinach with another generous pinch of salt, then drizzle the dressing on top and toss lightly.

4. Transfer to a chilled serving bowl. Serve at once, passing extra vinaigrette along.

Tomatillo Salsa Verde

MAKES 4 SERVINGS

Literally "little tomatoes," tomatillos arrive at the market when the fruit is still immature and has a very tart flavor, much different than its relative, the tomato. Native to Mexico and Central America, tomatillos were first cultivated by the ancient Aztecs. Their tart, piquant flavor is perfect for traditional salsa verde, which is served with everything from enchiladas and quesadillas to fried chicken and grilled fish.

Purple tomatillos are sweeter and can be eaten raw, whereas the classic green tomatillos have a sour, astringent taste best suited for salsa verde. Tomatillos self-seed so there's a mix of transplanted plants and self-seeded surprises at Jasper Meadows Farm.

olive oil
12 Jasper Meadows Farm tomatillos, husks peeled
½ cup chopped Valley View Farm Candy onion
2 cloves garlic
½ cup chopped cilantro leaves and stems
1 tablespoon fresh lime juice
2 Jackman Vineyards jalapeño or serrano peppers, stemmed, seeded, and chopped
kosher salt

1. Coat the bottom of a skillet with oil and heat on high heat. Place the tomatillos in the pan and sear on one side, then flip over and brown the other side. Remove from heat.

2. Place the cooked tomatillos, onion, garlic, cilantro, lime juice, and chile peppers in a blender or food processor and pulse until finely chopped and mixed. Season with salt to taste.

3. Cover and refrigerate until ready to serve.

"Tomato with a History" Sandwich on Gary's Bread

MAKES 2 SERVINGS

Thor Oechsner, Liz Brown, and Stef Senders of Wide Awake Bakery are responsible for some of the longest lines at the market, but of course, there's a good reason for that. Organic local grains are milled in small batches to produce each precious loaf, including the crusty "Gary's Bread," named for the late Gary Redmond, supporter of local farms and local economies.

Among the first heirloom tomatoes to arrive at the market from West Haven Farm is the colorful, whimsically named Berkeley Tie-Dye, a green fruit with red and yellow stripes. This vine-ripened tomato provides the sandwich we wait for all year. Accompany with enough napkins to catch the juice of the nourishing tomato and some of the mayonnaise that drips down your chin with each bite.

4 slices Wide Awake Bakery Gary's
  Bread
1 West Haven Farm heirloom tomato,
  ripe but firm
mayonnaise
kosher salt
freshly ground black pepper

1. Lightly toast the bread.

2. Core and cut the tomato into ⅛-inch slices.

3. Slather one side of each piece of toast with mayonnaise (more or less, as desired) and layer tomato slices on top of 2 slices of the toasted bread.

4. Season with salt and pepper to taste.

5. Top with the other slices of toast. Cut each sandwich in half diagonally.

Truffle Popcorn with Pecorino Romano Cheese

MAKES 4 SERVINGS

In Native American folklore, it was believed that corn kernels were inhabited by spirits. When the kernels were heated, the spirits grew angry and burst out of their homes in a puff of steam. Popcorn kernels have a hard exterior shell covering a soft, starchy center. The white starchy mass that is popcorn appears when the kernels explode and turn inside out.

It is said that the fragrant scent of truffles is a combination of the memories of lost youth and old love affairs. Infused with white truffles, the oil bathes popcorn with intense aromatics, enhanced with the tang of sheep's cheese and the spicy heat of freshly ground pepper.

1 tablespoon + ¼ cup extra-virgin olive oil
½ cup Rainbow Valley Ranch popping corn
¼ cup unsalted butter, melted
¼ cup white truffle oil
1 cup Pecorino Romano cheese, freshly grated
freshly ground black pepper

1. Heat 1 tablespoon of the oil in a large metal pot over medium-high heat.

2. Add 2 corn kernels to test the oil temperature, cover, keeping the lid slightly ajar, and cook until the kernels pop.

3. Add the remaining popping corn and cook with the lid slightly ajar, shaking the pot frequently, until all of the corn has popped and popping sound stops. Remove from heat.

4. Transfer the popcorn to a large serving bowl. Drizzle with butter and truffle oil, tossing to coat. Add cheese and pepper to taste, and toss to combine.

Zucchini Pronto

The secret to this summertime antipasto is a quick, ever-so-slight saute of young, tender zucchini, maintaining freshness and firmness as it mingles with toasted almonds and olive oil. For the finishing touch, it's draped with paper-thin sheets of Pecorino Romano cheese, shaved with a vegetable peeler. Add more nuts if you desire a higher almond-to-zucchini ratio.

3 tablespoons extra-virgin olive oil
2 tablespoons raw slivered almonds
1 medium Nook & Cranny Farm Safari
   zucchini, unpeeled, cut into 1½-inch
   matchsticks
squeezed juice of ½ lemon
1 tablespoon chopped parsley
kosher salt
freshly ground black pepper
6 to 8 paper-thin sheets Pecorino
   Romano cheese

1. Heat the oil on high heat in a large skillet. Add almonds to the pan and cook while stirring, until golden brown, about 1 to 2 minutes.

2. Add zucchini matchsticks to the pan, tossing with oil and almonds, about 1 minute. Keep the pan moving, ensuring the zucchini is completely coated in oil and almonds are fully mixed in.

3. Remove from heat. Add the lemon juice and parsley, season with salt and pepper to taste, and toss to coat.

4. To serve, quickly remove from the pan and divide between 2 warmed plates. Layer the cheese sheets over the top of each. Allow cheese to melt with the heat of the zucchini for 1 minute before serving.

MAIN DISHES

Dr. Baker's Cornell Barbecue Chicken

MAKES 6 SERVINGS

Created by Dr. Robert C. Baker, professor emeritus at the College of Agriculture and Life Sciences at Cornell, this is the original Chicken Coop recipe from Dr. Baker's legendary stand at the New York State Fair. The regional favorite is served throughout the summer at every kind of upstate community event, from Boy Scout fundraisers to church and fire department cookouts and county fairs.

2 cups Littletree Orchards apple cider vinegar
1 cup vegetable oil
1 Kingbird Farm chicken egg
3 tablespoons kosher salt
1 tablespoon poultry seasoning
½ teaspoon freshly ground black pepper
1 (3–3½ pound) Shannon Brock Farm broiler chicken, cut in half

1. Combine cider vinegar, oil, egg, salt, poultry seasoning, and pepper in a blender and puree until smooth.

2. Pour marinade into a resealable plastic bag. Add chicken halves, coat with marinade, squeeze out excess air, and seal the bag. Marinate in the refrigerator overnight.

3. Preheat outdoor grill for medium-high heat and lightly oil the grate.

4. Remove chicken halves from the bag and transfer to a paper towel–lined baking sheet. Pat chicken dry with more paper towels. Reserve marinade.

5. Place chicken, skin-side down, onto the preheated grill over direct heat. Grill for 2 minutes, then turn each piece, using a long-handled fork, brush with marinade, and move to indirect heat.

6. Continue to cook, turning often and basting with marinade (basting should be light at first and heavy near the end of the cooking period), until browned and meat is no longer pink in the center, about 45 minutes.

7. Test doneness by pulling the wing away from the body and using an instant meat thermometer. If the meat in this area splits easily and the thermometer reads at least 165 degrees F in the breast and thigh, the chicken is done.

8. Let rest for 5 to 10 minutes before slicing.

Grilled Bison Burgers with Havarti Cheese

MAKES 8 SERVINGS

An iconic American species, bison roam the pasture on part of 80-acre Glenwood Farms, overlooking Cayuga Lake. The Reynolds family—Greg, Evan, Alex, and Tammy—has delivered bison cuts and ground bison to the market since 2008. With a slightly sweeter flavor compared to ground beef, this simple preparation for bison burgers allows the earthy, mineral-rich flavors to shine through.

Old Chatham Creamery was founded in 1993 on the rolling hills of the Hudson Valley, and lucky for Ithaca marketgoers, purchased by Cornell dairy professor Dr. David Galton and relocated to nearby Groton. Milk for Old Chatham cheese comes from a flock of Laucune and East Friesian sheep, one of the largest flocks of its kind in America.

2 pounds Glenwood Farms ground
　bison
kosher salt
freshly ground black pepper
8 hamburger rolls
8 slices Old Chatham Creamery
　Havarti

1. Preheat grill to medium-high heat (about 400 degrees F).

2. Divide the bison and shape into 1/4-pound patties. Sprinkle each with salt and pepper.

3. Place burgers on the grill. Cook until the edges of the burgers brown, 3 to 5 minutes, then flip and cook another 3 to 5 minutes or until internal temperature reaches a minimum of 145 degrees F (160 degrees F for well-done).

4. Top each burger with a slice of cheese. Cover with the grill lid or a large heatproof bowl and continue to cook until the cheese has melted and the burgers are still slightly pink on the inside, about 3 minutes more. Remove from heat.

5. Toast rolls on the grill, open sides down. Serve burgers on the toasted rolls.

Grilled Shrimp with Green Cocktail Sauce

MAKES 4 SERVINGS

For the best grilled shrimp, marinate for an hour or so in a mixture of olive oil, sugar, onion powder, salt, and pepper. Thread closely together on a skewer, then cook fast and hot. The salt helps shrimp retain moisture, sugar helps with browning, and threading on skewers makes them easy to flip.

An alternative to traditional cocktail sauce, the green version is a puree of tangy, Jasper Meadows Farm tomatillos, garlic, and horseradish, plus a dose of green pepper hot sauce.

¼ cup extra-virgin olive oil
1 teaspoon granulated sugar
1 teaspoon onion powder
1 teaspoon kosher salt
½ teaspoon freshly ground black
   pepper
1 pound raw jumbo shrimp, peeled and
   deveined
green cocktail sauce*

1. In a wide shallow bowl, combine olive oil, sugar, onion powder, salt, and black pepper.

2. Add shrimp to bowl, and fold gently to coat shrimp evenly with the marinade. Cover and refrigerate for 2 to 3 hours.

3. Preheat outdoor grill for medium-high heat and lightly oil the grate.

4. When grill is hot, remove shrimp from fridge. Thread onto skewers, and grill for 3 to 4 minutes on each side.

5. Remove shrimp from skewers and arrange on a serving platter. Serve with cocktail sauce for dipping.

*For the green cocktail sauce:

1 pound Jasper Meadows Farm tomatillos, husked and cut
   into quarters
1 teaspoon Six Circles Farm Spanish Roja garlic clove, minced
1 tablespoon prepared horseradish
2 teaspoons green pepper hot sauce
kosher salt
freshly ground black pepper

1. In a food processor, combine all ingredients except salt and pepper. Puree until nearly smooth.

2. Scrape into a bowl and season with salt and pepper to taste.

3. Cover and refrigerate until ready to use.

Makes 2 cups

Guinea Egg and Cheese in a Bagel Hole

MAKES 2 SERVINGS

Native to the coastal countries of West Africa, Guinea fowl were introduced to Europe in the 1400s and arrived in America on slave ships together with African captives. Guinea eggs are slightly smaller than chicken eggs, with a deep golden-orange colored yolk and a rich, creamy flavor.

At Jasper Meadows Farm, Madi and Chuck Alridge decided to raise guinea hens because they serve a dual purpose both as tick eaters and layers of beautiful, delicious eggs. These teardrop-shaped, speckled eggs possess a hard shell that requires deliberate cracking. The hens lay their eggs from mid-May through September, preferring to hunker down during the colder months. Collecting these prized eggs becomes a daily Easter egg hunt on the farm, explains Madi, since their free-spirited nature leads them to roam and wander.

1 bagel, halved
1 tablespoon butter, softened
2 slices Snow Farm Creamery baby Swiss
2 Jasper Meadows Farm guinea hen eggs
sea salt
freshly ground black pepper
chives, chopped into chiffonade

1. Preheat oven to 375 degrees F and line a baking sheet with parchment paper.

2. Using a small biscuit cutter, cut out the center of the bagel to make the hole wider.

3. Brush the cut sides of the bagel with butter and place cut-side down on the baking sheet.

4. Press slice of cheese into each bagel hole.

5. Crack an egg into the center of each bagel hole, on top of the cheese slices.

6. Season the eggs with salt and pepper and place in the oven for about 10 to 15 minutes, depending on how you like your eggs cooked. Remove from oven.

7. Transfer to serving plates and garnish with chives.

Pan-Seared Cod with Strawberry Salsa

MAKES 4 SERVINGS

"Strawberries are full of love and happiness," writes Anthony T. Hincks. Dickens strawberries, a hybrid variety developed in Cornell's berry breeding program, produce large fruits with vibrant colors that maintain peak flavor for longer than most heritage varieties. The June-bearing strawberries grown on Stick and Stone Farm are firm, so they hold up especially well in a delicious fruit salsa.

sea salt

freshly ground black pepper

4 cod fillets (or other white fish)

1 pound Stick and Stone Farm Dickens strawberries, stems removed, chopped

¼ cup Valley View Farm Candy onion, chopped

1 Jackman Vineyards serrano pepper, seeded, finely chopped

1 handful fresh cilantro sprigs, finely chopped

squeezed juice of ½ lime

2 tablespoons butter

1. Salt and pepper both sides of the cod fillets. Set aside.

2. Combine strawberries, onion, serrano peppers, cilantro, and lime juice. Set aside.

3. Add one tablespoon of butter to a large skillet and melt over medium-high heat. Place two of the cod fillets in the skillet and cook for 5 to 6 minutes on each side or until it reaches an internal temperature of 145 degrees F.

4. Remove from the skillet and repeat with butter and the other two fillets.

5. Place cod fillets on each of 4 warmed dinner plates. Top each with a generous portion of the strawberry salsa.

Peperonata Chicken

MAKES 4 SERVINGS

Peperonata, from the Italian word peperone, *meaning "sweet peppers," is the rustic stew of Southern Italy, traditionally from Calabria, the "toe" of the Italian "boot." In a market-inspired version, sweet summer Italian peppers grown on Jackman Vineyards are roasted with garlic, tomatoes, and olives and served with free-range chicken breasts from Just a Few Acres Farm, a forty-five-acre, seventh-generation, diversified livestock farm in Lansing.*

4 Jackman Vineyards Italian sweet peppers, cored, seeded, and thinly sliced

5 Six Circles Farm Spanish Roja garlic cloves, thinly sliced

4 tablespoons extra-virgin olive oil

kosher salt

freshly ground black pepper

12 ounces Jackman Vineyards cherry tomatoes

½ cup green olives, pitted and chopped

1 tablespoon red wine vinegar

4 Just a Few Acres Farm boneless, skinless chicken breasts

extra-virgin olive oil

1. Heat oven to 425 degrees F. In a large baking dish, combine peppers, garlic, and olive oil. Season with salt and pepper to taste, toss to combine, and arrange in an even layer. Roast until softened, about 20 minutes. Stir in tomatoes, olives, and vinegar.

2. In a large bowl, coat chicken with olive oil and season with salt and pepper. Place breasts on top of pepper mixture. Roast until chicken is cooked through and peperonata is tender, about 20 to 25 minutes.

3. Arrange chicken breasts on each of 4 warmed plates. Top each with a generous portion of the peperonata.

Raw Zucchini "Zoodles" with Garlic Scape Pesto

MAKES 4 SERVINGS

At the Nook & Cranny Farm stand, a hybrid zucchini variety called Safari is easily recognizable by its stunning dark green skin with white stripes. It has a mild flavor with nuances of black peppercorn and nutty undertones.

This is a satisfying dish when it's too hot to cook. To make zucchini noodles, a julienne peeler slices zucchinis into the thin, delicate noodles, and a mandoline allows you to vary the thickness to create flat noodles. The best tool is a spiralizer. Simply cut off the ends of a zucchini, place it next to the blade, and spin.

4 medium Nook & Cranny Safari
   zucchini, ends trimmed
garlic scape pesto*
extra-virgin olive oil

1. Use a julienne peeler, spiralizer, or mandoline to slice the zucchini into noodles.

2. Place zucchini noodles in a large bowl. Toss with pesto. Drizzle with olive oil.

3. Pass family style around the table.

*For the garlic scape pesto:

12 Six Circles Farm garlic scapes, diced
½ cup chopped basil
⅓ cup cashews
½ cup extra-virgin olive oil
½ cup grated Parmesan cheese
½ teaspoon lemon juice
sea salt
freshly cracked black pepper

1. In a food processor, blend the garlic scapes and basil for 30 seconds.

2. Add the nuts and blend for another 30 seconds.

3. Slowly drizzle in the olive oil.

4. Add the parmesan cheese, lemon juice, and salt and pepper to taste.

DESSERTS

Boysenberry Fool

MAKES 4 SERVINGS

The purple-red boysenberry, a cross between a blackberry and raspberry, was developed by a California horti-culturist named Rudolph Boysen in the 1920s. Delicate in texture, the fruit is both sweet and tart, the proportions depending on ripeness.

Ely Fruit Farms boysenberries have a brief growing season and a short selling season at the market. When selecting the fruit, look for plump berries, and since they don't keep well, eat them quickly.

1 pint Ely Fruit Farms boysenberries
2 tablespoons granulated sugar
2 teaspoons vanilla extract
1 cup heavy cream
2 tablespoons confectioners' sugar

1. Place the boysenberries in a medium bowl and sprinkle with the granulated sugar, then drizzle with the vanilla. Toss lightly to evenly coat. Allow to steep for 10 minutes, then mash the berries until they release their juices and form a thick pulp.

2. Combine the heavy cream and confectioners' sugar in another medium bowl. Use an electric stand or hand mixer to whip the cream to medium peaks.

3. Pour the berry mixture over the cream and use a spatula to gently fold until combined.

4. Scoop into 4 individual chilled goblets and serve immediately.

Chester Platt's Cherry "Sunday"

MAKES 4 SERVINGS

In 1892, the soda fountain menu at Platt & Colt Pharmacy on State Street in Ithaca offered a dish of ice cream for a nickel, and local Unitarian minister John M. Scott often stopped in after Sunday services for a plain scoop of vanilla. One visit in particular proved memorable. "On a whim," proprietor Chester C. Platt dipped Reverend Scott's ice cream into a champagne saucer, poured cherry syrup over the top, then added a whole candied cherry. As the two men pondered what to call the new concoction, Scott proposed that it be named after the day it was invented.

Cherry harvest often marks what feels like the true beginning of summer at Black Diamond Farm. A dark burgundy variety called Balaton puts the cherry on top of the dessert invented in Ithaca.

cherry syrup*
4 scoops vanilla ice cream**
1 cup whipped cream
4 whole Black Diamond Farm Balaton
   cherries with stems

1. Ladle 2 ounces of syrup into the bottoms of 4 chilled tulip dishes.

2. Place 1 scoop of the ice cream on top of the syrup, then ladle a generous portion of the syrup over the ice cream.

3. Top each with whipped cream and garnish with a whole cherry.

*For the cherry syrup:

1 cup water, divided
1½ tablespoons cornstarch
3½ cups Black Diamond Farm Balaton cherries, pitted,
   stems removed
3–4 tablespoons sugar
½ teaspoon vanilla extract

1. Measure ½ cup of water. In a separate small dish, combine cornstarch with a few spoonfuls of the measured water and mix until smooth. Mix in the remaining ½ cup of water. Set aside.

2. Place cherries in a small saucepan. Add cornstarch slurry and sugar. Set pan on the stove over medium-high heat and cook until sauce has thickened, stirring frequently.

3. Once thickened, remove sauce from heat and stir in extract. Transfer to an airtight container and refrigerate until ready to use.

Makes 2½ cups

(continued)

**For the vanilla ice cream:

2½ cups Crosswinds Creamery milk, divided
½ cup sugar
pinch of salt
3 tablespoons cornstarch
2 teaspoons vanilla extract

1. Combine 2 cups milk, sugar, and salt in a saucepan over medium-low heat.

2. In a bowl, blend cornstarch and remaining milk. Add mixture to the pan. Cook, stirring, until it begins to thicken, about 5 minutes. Reduce heat to very low and stir until thick, about 5 more minutes. Stir in vanilla extract.

3. Chill in the fridge. When completely cool, pour into an ice cream machine and freeze according to manufacturer's instructions.

4. Transfer the finished ice cream to an airtight container and place in the freezer until ready to serve.

Glenhaven Farm Blueberry Muffins

MAKES 16 MUFFINS

At Glenhaven Farm, John Tamburello nurtures eleven acres of Blue Crop and Elliot blueberries, both abundant "highbush" varieties, transported to the market every summer since 2004. To keep birds from munching on his blueberry crop, John plays recordings of the cries and calls of birds of prey at random intervals every day during peak season.

Blueberry season lasts only a few precious weeks, from mid-July to late August, and the appearance of fresh-picked blueberries at the Glenhaven Farm stand inspires plump, crusty-topped muffins bursting with sweet, fruity flavor. Blueberries are the sturdiest berry and keep fine in the fridge for a week or more.

3½ cups all-purpose flour, sifted
2 tablespoons baking powder
¾ cup sugar
5 eggs, slightly beaten
½ cup Crosswinds Creamery milk
5 ounces unsalted butter, melted and
    cooled
6 cups Glenhaven Farm blueberries

1. Preheat oven to 400 degrees F.

2. Mix all dry ingredients together. Stir in eggs, milk, and butter (do not overmix). Stir in berries.

3. Grease the top of large muffin tins. Insert paper cups and spoon batter to the top of each.

4. Place muffin tins on the middle rack of the hot oven. Bake until muffins are golden brown, about 20 to 25 minutes. Remove from tins and allow to cool.

Outdoor Grilled Peaches with Honey and Butter

MAKES 4 SERVINGS

"An apple is an excellent thing," writes George Du Maurier, "until you have tried a peach!" Fresh-picked Loring freestone peaches from Ely Fruit Farms are large, sunset-hued fuzzy gems with sweet, fragrant, yellow flesh and firm texture, ideal for summer grilling.

Derived from the nectar of flowers, honey has been used to describe everything from sweetness to sensuality and even as a metaphor for goodness. Heat from the grill transforms a drizzle of honey into a sweet, smoky glaze.

4 Ely Fruit Farms Loring peaches,
   halved and pitted
grapeseed oil, for brushing
4 tablespoons salted butter
Bright Raven Apiary Midsummer
   honey, for drizzling

1. Heat grill to medium.

2. Brush the cut side of each peach with oil. Place the peaches cut-side down directly on the hot grill. Cook, about 3 to 5 minutes, covered, until the peaches feel slightly softened. Remove from heat.

3. Arrange the peaches, cut-side up, on a serving platter. Dot the top of each with butter and drizzle with honey.

Panna Cotta with Black Currant Coulis

MAKES 8 SERVINGS

Originating in the Piedmont region of Northern Italy, panna cotta (meaning "cooked cream") is a traditional spoon dessert with a velvety texture, an ideal match for the flavors of just-picked fruit.

John Reynolds and Shannon O'Connor of Daring Drake Farm began growing black currants after visits to Europe in the 1990s. Widely grown in the Old World, black currants are the most intensely colored and flavored of all currants, tart and aromatic, at their best in midsummer, providing each bite of the delicate dessert with a harmonious blend of earthiness and sweetness.

1 envelope unflavored gelatin
2 tablespoons cold water
2 cups heavy cream
1 cup half-and-half
⅓ cup sugar
1½ teaspoons vanilla extract
black currant coulis*

1. In a small saucepan, sprinkle gelatin over water and allow to soften. Heat gelatin mixture over low heat until gelatin dissolves and remove pan from heat.

2. In a large saucepan, bring cream, half-and-half, and sugar to a boil over moderately high heat, stirring. Remove pan from heat and stir in gelatin mixture and vanilla extract.

3. Divide cream mixture among 8 ramekins and cool to room temperature. Chill for several hours or overnight.

4. Dip each ramekin into a bowl of hot water for a few seconds. Run a thin knife around the edge of each ramekin and invert onto the center of 8 small plates.

5. Just before serving, spoon a portion of the coulis over each panna cotta.

*For the black currant coulis:

3 cups Daring Drake Farm black currants
¼ cup powdered sugar
1 teaspoon fresh lemon juice

1. In a food processor or blender, add black currants and powdered sugar. Pulse until fruit is pureed.

2. Strain puree through a fine-mesh strainer, pressing to extract all the juice. Discard the pulp.

3. Stir in the lemon juice and add additional powdered sugar to taste.

Pears Poached in Cabernet Franc

MAKES 6 SERVINGS

The Bartlett is a very old European pear known primarily as "Williams" throughout Europe. First planted in America on an estate in Dorchester, Massachusetts, later acquired by merchant Enoch Bartlett, the trees were thought to be seedlings and named after Bartlett. By the time anyone realized the Bartlett pear was the same as the Williams pear, the name had stuck.

The village of Burdett is home to both Ely Fruit Farms and Damiani Wine Cellars.

6 firm but ripe Ely Fruit Farms Bartlett pears
1 (750 ml) bottle Damiani Cabernet Franc
1¼ cups sugar
1 teaspoon whole black peppercorns
6 whole cloves
1 cinnamon stick
vanilla ice cream (see page 77)

1. Using a vegetable peeler, peel the pears top to bottom, leaving them whole, with stems attached and the core intact.

2. Put the pears in a large, wide pot in one layer. Add the wine, sugar, and spices. Cover and bring to a boil, then reduce heat to a slow simmer, and cook for about 30 minutes. Remove from heat and set pears aside, leaving the liquid in the pot.

3. Heat the poaching liquid over high and boil down until it is reduced by half. Cool in the fridge.

4. To serve, place a pear in each of 6 small bowls, add a scoop of ice cream, and spoon the red wine syrup on top.

ITHACA FARMERS MARKET HISTORY: 1988

In 1988, it was Ann Rider again, this time in her role as market secretary, who led prolonged negotiations with local officials for a new permanent home, the lease of 5.8 acres of city-owned lakefront property at Steamboat Landing, once the site of Ithaca's waterway transportation hub. After completion in 1828 of the Cayuga-Seneca Canal, connecting the lakes to the Erie Canal, commercial steamboats arrived here to collect produce from local growers and transferred cargo for delivery to downstate markets.

The task of designing a permanent structure to satisfy the desires and aspirations of market vendors was entrusted to architect Stephen Gibian. Earlier locations had previously determined that sellers required ten-by-twelve-feet spaces and that a twenty-feet-wide customer aisle between parallel rows of multiple bays avoided congestion. Despite Ithaca's unpredictable weather, the preference for maintaining an open-air facility was nearly unanimous.

A formal groundbreaking took place at Steamboat Landing on July 1, 1989, and the land was cleared by farmers using their own equipment.

Gibian's design called for a lofty, *T*-shaped pavilion, providing a long hallway down its center line. The interior space would be spanned with branchlike, site-built trusses; clerestory openings would allow plenty of daylight, and cupolas would provide efficient air circulation.

Building a Dream, Pavilion Taking Shape, 1990

With reference to historic European public markets, including Halles Centrale and Richelieu Market Hall, the plan was ambitious yet ingeniously cost efficient. But its accomplishment depended on a collaboration of resources.

Financed through local fundraising and grants written by Monika Roth from the New York State Department of Agriculture and Markets, the pavilion was built in phases, entirely by volunteer labor—vendors, their families, and supporters from the community, with Gibian as the project lead.

Work began after Saturday market hours with jobs assigned in teams. Each section was completed by the time the market opened on the following weekend. This was truly a local affair, and even the building materials were relatively local. Nearly all lumber was rough cut from nearby Hemlock and other hardwood species and processed by a sawmill in Greene.

Jim Cummins (at top), Vendor and Construction Manager, with Steve Gibian, Architect, 1990

Raise High the Roof Beam, Volunteer Labor, 1990

The Market at Steamboat Landing, Mission Accomplished, 1991

Growing from the seed of an idea and just a handful of vendors, the Ithaca Farmers Market finally had a permanent home, and the time was exactly right. The slow food movement had taken hold in response to the growth of fast food and other changes in the food system, and the Ithaca model became a case study in reducing environmental impact of food production, respecting seasonality, and supporting local growers and culinary traditions.

"Teamwork is the ability to work together toward a common vision," writes Andrew Carnegie. "It is the fuel that allows common people to attain uncommon results."

FALL

*For man, autumn is a time of harvest,
of gathering together. For nature, it is a
time of sowing, of scattering abroad.*

—Edwin Way Teale

BEVERAGES AND COCKTAILS

Concord Grape Juice "Transfusion"

MAKES 1 DRINK

"The juice of the grape is the liquid quintessence of concentrated sunbeams," writes English novelist and poet Thomas Love Peacock.

The Concord grape was first propagated from wild seedlings by a farmer named Ephraim Wales Bull in Concord, Massachusetts, in 1849. Concords were planted in western New York during the 1870s, where the climate and soil proved to be ideal for growing the distinctive dark purple grapes. Marie Ely Baumgardner, "the Grape Lady," has brought farm-grown Concord fruit, juice, jams, and jellies to the market for more than forty years.

The Concord Grape Juice Transfusion cocktail is light and quaffable, with vodka providing the booze, ginger ale the effervescence, and Concord grape juice the sweetness.

3 ounces vodka
1½ ounces Ely Fruit Farms Concord
   grape juice
¼ ounce fresh lime juice
ginger ale
lime wedge

1. Combine vodka, grape juice, and lime juice in a tall glass filled with cracked ice.

2. Top up with ginger ale and garnish with lime wedge.

Naked in Moravia

MAKES 1 DRINK

Regulars at the market since 2018, Joe Steuer and Steve Daughhetee of the New York Cider Company craft small-batch ciders on Ithaca's West Hill, with apples sourced from their own Hayts Road orchard, from nearby growers, and foraged from wild and abandoned trees.

The partners have a favorite story, the one about a market customer who asked if they might be interested in the old apple trees at his nudist colony, the Empire Haven Nudist Park in Moravia. It seems the property surrounding the colony contains the remnants of a large pre-Prohibition seedling cider orchard, and in 2020, Steve introduced Naturist, a full-bodied blend made with the distinctive apples gathered there. This riff on a classic hard cider cocktail combines the bracing tartness of the cider with deeply flavored fall honey from Waid's Apiaries.

1 ounce scotch

¾ ounce Aperol

½ ounce Waid's Apiaries buckwheat honey

½ ounce fresh lemon juice

3 ounces New York Cider Company Naturist hard apple cider

lemon peel

1. Combine scotch, Aperol, honey, and lemon juice in a mixing glass filled with cracked ice. Shake vigorously and transfer contents to a tall highball glass.

2. Top up with the cider. Express lemon peel over the glass, rub it around the rim, and drop in.

Paris between the Wars

MAKES 1 DRINK

This cider cocktail, created by Off-Broadway performer-turned-mixologist Abigail Gullo, combines the lively effervescence and robust tannins of the cider with the bitterness of Campari and smokiness of scotch.

Porter's Perfection is a British bittersweet cider apple from the 1800s, grown on the Black Diamond Farm orchard in Trumansburg, and crafted into a varietal hard cider by renowned pomologist Ian Merwin. "Shin Hollow" pays tribute to the old name of the village of Trumansburg, supposedly a reference to the bumps and bruises tipplers sustained on their way home, weaving in and out among the tree stumps.

¾ ounce Campari
¾ ounce scotch
½ ounce fresh lemon juice
½ ounce simple syrup
3 ounces Black Diamond Shin Hollow
   apple cider, chilled
lemon peel

1. Shake the first 4 ingredients in a shaker with ice until chilled.

2. Strain into a chilled flute. Top with the cider.

3. Express lemon peel over the glass, rub it around the rim, and drop in.

SALADS AND SMALL PLATES

Baked Sweet Potatoes with Tatsoi Pesto

MAKES 4 SERVINGS

Jackman Vineyards, Alex Jackman's intensively managed vegetable farm, is located just north of where Indian Creek flows into Cayuga Lake northwest of Ithaca.

Baking is the time-honored method for cooking sweet potatoes, and a mainstay of late November family meals. Earthy, garlicky pesto creates a satisfying contrast with the natural sweetness of hyper-local sweet potatoes. For consistently soft and sweet baked sweet potatoes, shop for small or medium sweet potatoes because they tend to be less starchy.

4 Jackman Vineyards sweet potatoes
olive oil
tatsoi pesto*

1. Preheat oven to 425 degrees F. On a baking sheet lined with aluminum foil, prick potatoes with a fork. Rub with olive oil.

2. Bake until tender, about 45 to 50 minutes. Remove from oven.

3. Split the tops open with a knife and top each with a heaping tablespoon of pesto.

*For the tatsoi pesto:

4 cups chopped Oxbow Farm tatsoi
⅓ cup pine nuts
3 cloves Six Circles Farm German Red garlic, minced
½ cup freshly grated Parmesan
½ cup extra-virgin olive oil
sea salt
freshly ground black pepper

1. Place the tatsoi leaves and pine nuts into the bowl of a food processor and pulse several times.

2. Add the garlic and cheese and pulse several more times.

3. While the food processor is running, slowly add the olive oil in a steady stream. Stop occasionally to scrape down the sides of the food processor.

4. Season with salt and pepper to taste. Transfer to an airtight container and refrigerate until ready to use.

Brussels Sprouts Carpaccio with Goat Cheese

MAKES 4 SERVINGS

The miniature green cabbages we call brussels sprouts originated in the capital city of Belgium. As Brussels experienced dramatic growth during the Industrial Revolution, local farmers had trouble finding space for growing crops. They bred this variety of cabbage to grow vertically, requiring less farmland.

This is the time of year when you see folks carrying nearly two-foot-long stalks of brussels sprouts home from the market, each adorned with as many as two dozen baby cabbages.

In this version of the traditional Italian appetizer, the crunch and color of raw brussels sprouts combine with Old Chatham Creamery Lumberjack, a bloomy-rind goat's milk cheese crafted in the Bucheron style, native to the Loire Valley in France. Notes of citrus and earthiness temper the bitterness of the sprouts.

12 ounces Stick and Stone Farm brussels sprouts
6 ounces Old Chatham Creamery goat cheese, shaved
2 teaspoons capers, rinsed
kosher salt
freshly ground black pepper
extra-virgin olive oil

1. Remove the outer layers from the brussels sprouts. Slice and shred the inner portion of each sprout.

2. Spread the shredded sprouts among 4 chilled serving plates. Divide the shaved cheese among each. Top each with capers, season with salt and pepper to taste, then drizzle with olive oil to finish.

Confetti Kale

MAKES 4 SERVINGS

Beautiful blue-green, thick-crinkled Italian heirloom kale leaves provide the roughage in a colorful rhapsody of vibrant seasonal ingredients.

Smaller than bell peppers, Italian sweet peppers are elongated, tapered, and slightly curved with a glossy, waxy skin. Their gentle flavor adds zest to this savory side dish. Sweet corn adds a burst of color and texture, and garlic provides spicy gusto.

2 tablespoons extra-virgin olive oil
1 clove Six Circles Farm Spanish Roja garlic, thinly sliced
½ cup Jackman Vineyards Italian sweet peppers, chopped
¾ cup Mandeville Farm sweet corn kernels
6 cups West Haven Farm Tuscan kale, washed, dried, and chopped into confetti
kosher salt
freshly ground black pepper

1. In a large skillet, heat the oil over medium heat and saute the garlic for about 30 seconds. Add the peppers and stir for five more minutes.

2. Add corn kernels and kale and cook, just until kale is wilted, stirring constantly. Season with salt and pepper to taste.

3. Transfer to a warmed serving bowl and pass family style around the table.

Irish Colcannon

MAKES 4 SERVINGS

"Food is the most primitive form of comfort," writes columnist Sheila Graham, and colcannon is Irish comfort food at its most comforting. Originating in the peasant kitchens of Ireland, this rich, hearty, and deeply satisfying side dish marries creamy mashed potatoes and tender sauteed cabbage with a melting pool of butter resting like a golden lake on top.

Developed by cabbage breeder Don Reed in Cortland, Storage #4 cabbages have solid heads, delicious, crisp leaves, mature just prior to the fall frosts, and are capable of long-term storage into the winter months.

4 Sabol's Farm Keuka Gold potatoes, peeled and cut into chunks
kosher salt
1 stick butter, plus more for serving
3 cups chopped Nook & Cranny Farm Storage #4 cabbage
heavy cream

1. Put the chopped potatoes in a large pot of boiling water. Add a pinch of salt to season. Boil until the potatoes are fork-tender, about 15 minutes. Drain in a colander.

2. In a large skillet over medium heat, add butter and cabbage and cook until cabbage is tender.

3. Return potatoes to the large pot and mash with a potato masher, adding heavy cream as needed to reach a smooth consistency.

4. Gently fold the mashed potatoes and cabbage together.

5. To serve, make a depression in the middle of the mashed potatoes and put a knob of butter in it.

Mostarda di Frutta and Gouda Plate

MAKES 4 TO 6 SERVINGS

"Give me juicy autumnal fruit, ripe and red from the orchard," writes Walt Whitman.

This traditional Northern Italian condiment is based on sweet, richly flavored Chestnut Crab apples from Black Diamond Farm. The mostarda is made by caramelizing the apples with sugar and mustard oil. In this party tray version, the candied fruit is served with Old Chatham Creamery's buttery, nutty Three-Milk Gouda, made with the milk of sheep, cows, and goats.

3 lemons

4 Black Diamond Farm Chestnut Crab apples, cored, peeled, cut into slices

1 cup sugar

1 tablespoon mustard oil

1 block Old Chatham Creamery Three-Milk Gouda, sliced

Carr's Rosemary Crackers (or other crackers)

1. Cut one lemon into thin slices. Juice the other two lemons. Put the sliced apples in a bowl and pour sugar and lemon juice over them. Cover with plastic wrap and allow the apples to soak in the syrup overnight.

2. The next day, remove the juice from the apples and pour it into a saucepan. Bring to a boil and cook for about 5 minutes. Pour sauce over the apples once again while boiling. Repeat the procedure 2 or 3 times over the next 24 hours. After the last boil, stir in the mustard oil and cool in the fridge.

3. To serve, transfer the mostarda to a serving dish. Place on the center of a platter. Arrange lemon slices, cheese slices, and crackers around the platter.

Roasted Brussels Sprouts with Apple Cider Vinegar Drizzle

MAKES 4 SERVINGS

For this rustic fall dish, simply roasted brussels sprouts are drizzled with fragrant apple cider vinegar. This recipe calls for vinegar that's infused with rosemary and sage, but choose your own favorite from the range of creative vinegars handcrafted by Amara Steinkraus at Littletree Orchards.

4 tablespoons extra-virgin olive oil

1 pound Stick and Stone Farm brussels sprouts, sliced in half, top to bottom

4 cloves Six Circles Farm Spanish Roja garlic, peeled

kosher salt

freshly ground black pepper

1 tablespoon Littletree Orchards rosemary-sage-infused apple cider vinegar

1. Heat oven to 400 degrees F.

2. Heat oil in a cast-iron pan over medium-high heat. Add sprouts (cut-side down) and garlic.

3. Cook until sprouts begin to brown on the bottom. Transfer to oven and roast, about 15 to 20 minutes, shaking pan once or twice during cooking to roll the sprouts. Remove from heat.

4. Transfer to a warm serving bowl, season with salt and pepper to taste. Drizzle with apple cider vinegar, and pass family style around the table.

Roasted Butternut Squash Hash

MAKES 4 SERVINGS

In 1944, Charles Legget of Middlesex County, Massachusetts, crossed pumpkin and gooseneck squash varieties. The result was named "butternut" for its smooth-as-butter texture and nutty taste.

Shop for a squash that has a solid beige color on the outside without any cuts, soft spots, or punctures. The warm, earthy, and sweet notes of cinnamon add a layer of complexity to the dish.

1 Mandeville Farm butternut squash, peeled
2 tablespoons olive oil
2 cloves Six Circles Farm Spanish Roja garlic, minced
½ teaspoon ground cinnamon
sea salt
freshly ground black pepper

1. Preheat oven to 400 degrees F.

2. Cut squash in half lengthwise; scoop out and discard seeds. Slice into 1-inch cubes.

3. Combine butternut squash cubes, olive oil, and garlic in a large bowl and toss until well coated. Season with cinnamon and salt and pepper to taste. Arrange in a single layer on a baking sheet.

4. Roast in the oven until squash is lightly browned and tender when pierced with a fork, about 25 to 30 minutes.

5. Transfer to a warmed serving bowl and pass family style around the table.

Vichy Carrot "Cure"

MAKES 4 SERVINGS

Vichy, a spa town halfway between Paris and Montpellier, was famous for its therapeutic mineral water, and during the eighteenth century, carrots were served at many of the local restaurants, regarded as an important part of the overall "cure." Carrots were prescribed as a stomach tonic and believed to improve eyesight.

Parisian carrots, a very old French heirloom variety, are favorites of European chefs. You can't miss them at the Shagbark Gardens stand. They are small, globe- to top-shaped, and bright orange.

1 pound Shagbark Gardens Parisian carrots, peeled and sliced into ½-inch coins
2 tablespoons butter
1 teaspoon sugar
kosher salt
freshly ground black pepper
squeezed juice of 1 lemon
chives, chopped into chiffonade

1. Combine carrots, butter, sugar, and a pinch of salt and pepper in a saucepan.

2. Cover with cold water and boil until the water has evaporated and carrots are tender. Stir in lemon juice.

3. Transfer to a warmed serving dish. Scatter chives over top and pass family style around the table.

Whole Roasted "Music" Garlic

MAKES 4 SERVINGS

Six Circles Farm, located in the geographical center of the Finger Lakes, grows vegetables in the heart of wine country. Among eighty varieties of vegetables, fruit, and herbs, the Eisman family's main crop is garlic, delivering versatile, tasty, and seductive hardnecks to the market since 2003.

Music is a Porcelain variety of garlic, visually compelling and prized for its huge, plump cloves with true garlic flavor and easy-to-peel wrappers, making them a favorite in the kitchen. It's been said that happiness begins, geographically, where garlic is used in cooking, so this locally grown hardneck variety—one that becomes almost ambrosial after roasting—helps to make Ithaca a more joyful place.

4 whole Six Circles Farm Music garlic
   heads
extra-virgin olive oil
½ loaf Wide Awake Bakery Gary's
   Bread, sliced

1. Preheat oven to 400 degrees F.

2. Peel and discard the papery outer layer of the whole garlic head.

3. Using a sharp knife, cut ½ inch from the top of the cloves.

4. Place garlic heads in a muffin tin, cut side up. Drizzle a tablespoon of olive oil over each exposed head and cover each bulb with aluminum foil.

5. Bake for 30 to 40 minutes, or until the cloves feel soft when pressed. Remove from oven and allow to cool.

6. Squeeze out the softened garlic from the peel, mash, and spread over the bread slices.

Wilted Spinach Scented with Garlic

MAKES 4 SERVINGS

According to a French proverb, "Spinach is the broom of the stomach." A nutritional powerhouse high in fiber, spinach improves digestion and helps eliminate toxins from the body.

Among the forty types of vegetables and hundreds of varieties grown at Nook & Cranny Farm in Caroline, Kolibri is a vigorous, semi-savory hybrid spinach with slightly curled leaves with a medium-dark green, smooth surface. It gets treated to a quick saute in partnership with garlic for a savory side dish. A pinch or two of nutmeg gives the palate a nudge.

16 ounces Nook & Cranny Farm
  Kolibri spinach
¼ cup extra-virgin olive oil
3 cloves Six Circles Farm Spanish Roja
  garlic, peeled and sliced paper thin
ground or freshly grated nutmeg
sea salt
freshly ground black pepper

1. Pick spinach free of large stems, and wash and drain in a colander.

2. Heat the olive oil in large skillet over medium heat. Add spinach in bunches, turning and wilting leaves in the pan. Cook the spinach until just wilted, about 1 to 2 minutes. Halfway through, toss in the garlic and continue adding the remaining spinach. Remove from heat. Season with nutmeg and salt and pepper to taste.

3. Transfer to a warmed serving dish and pass family style around the table.

MAIN DISHES

Chicken Margherita with Mortar-and-Pestle Pesto Genovese

MAKES 4 SERVINGS

In 1889, chef Raffaele Esposito created a pizza in honor of Italy's unification, with the three toppings—basil, mozzarella, and tomato—representing the green, white, and red of the Italian flag, and named after the queen of Italy, Margherita of Savoy. The three-ingredient mix has become the most recognizable symbol of Italian food culture.

With glossy, dark green leaves and fragrant, distinctively warm, spicy flavors, Genovese basil is the best variety for pesto. The word pesto *itself is a derivation of the Italian word for "pounded," so for the sake of authenticity, it should be made with a mortar and pestle.*

4 Just a Few Acres Farm boneless
   chicken breasts
sea salt
freshly ground black pepper
2 tablespoons olive oil
1 teaspoon dried oregano
4 slices mozzarella
"mortar and pestle" pesto Genovese*

1. In a large bowl combine chicken, salt and pepper, olive oil, and oregano. Toss to combine.

2. Grill chicken over medium-high heat for about 6 to 8 minutes on each side until cooked through. Top each piece of chicken with a slice of mozzarella and cook another minute or so until melted.

3. Transfer a cheese-topped chicken breast onto each of 4 warmed dinner plates. Top each breast with about 2 heaping tablespoons of the pesto.

*For the "mortar and pestle" pesto Genovese:

3 Six Circles Farm Spanish Roja garlic cloves, peeled
¾ teaspoon sea salt
4 cups packed basil, blanched briefly in boiling water and
   shocked in ice water
½ cup extra-virgin olive oil
½ cup grated Parmesan
¼ cup pine nuts, toasted

1. Combine the garlic and salt in a mortar and pound with a pestle into a smooth paste. Coarsely chop the basil leaves, then add a handful at a time to the garlic mixture, grinding in a circular motion until each batch of leaves is incorporated.

2. Once well mashed, pound in the olive oil, adding a spoonful at a time until well incorporated.

3. Pound in the cheese then the pine nuts. Continue mashing for a few minutes until the pesto is as smooth as possible.

Kale and Spaghetti "Magic and Pasta"

MAKES 4 SERVINGS

The village farms of Tuscany gave birth to the unique heirloom kale called Cavolo Nero. In this popular Italian dish, the Tuscan kale leaves, even when cooked and combined with pasta, retain their firm structure. According to legendary Italian filmmaker Federico Fellini, "Life is a combination of magic and pasta."

The walnut is one of the hardest nuts to crack open. If you don't have a nutcracker, place each walnut on a flat surface. With the pointy end facing up, gently strike the walnut with a hammer. As the shell cracks open along the axis, pull it apart.

½ cup Sabol's Farm walnuts, roughly chopped

8 ounces whole wheat spaghetti or other long pasta

1½ tablespoons extra-virgin olive oil

2 Valley View Farm onions, thinly sliced

2 large bunches West Haven Farm Tuscan kale, stems removed and chopped

4 cloves Six Circles Farm Spanish Roja garlic, minced

1 (14-ounce) can diced tomatoes in their juices

⅔ cup Treleaven Dry Riesling

red pepper flakes

kosher salt

freshly ground black pepper

freshly grated Parmesan cheese

1. Heat a skillet over medium-low heat. Add the walnuts, stirring frequently, until golden brown, about 5 minutes. Set aside.

2. Bring a large pot of salted water to a boil. Cook pasta until al dente according to package directions.

3. Meanwhile, heat the olive oil in a large skillet over medium-high. Add the sliced onions and saute until tender, about 8 to 10 minutes, stirring frequently. Add the kale and saute for 4 to 5 minutes until wilted. Add the garlic and cook for 30 seconds. Stir in the tomatoes in their juices, wine, red pepper flakes, and salt and pepper to taste.

4. Bring the mixture to a boil, then reduce the heat to medium-low. Cover the pan and let simmer, stirring frequently, until the kale is soft and the tomatoes break down; about 3 to 5 minutes.

5. Add the cooked pasta to the skillet and stir to coat.

6. To serve, divide the pasta mix among 4 warmed dishes. Top each with toasted walnuts and a dusting of Parmesan.

Maple-Apple French Toast

MAKES 4 SERVINGS

In France, the dish is christened pain perdu, *meaning "lost bread," or bread that would otherwise be fed to the birds. Other countries have their own terms:* pafese *in Austria and Bavaria,* torrija *in Spain,* arme ritter *("poor knights") in Germany, and gypsy toast in England. In the spirit of American enterprise, Joseph French, an inn-keeper in Albany, New York, introduced the recipe in 1724, providing a lasting name for the classic comfort food.*

Apple picking is an annual rite of fall, a throwback to a simpler time when people weren't so disconnected from the source of their daily sustenance. If you don't get the chance to pick your own apples up at Littletree Orchards in Newfield, visit the Littletree stand at the market. There you'll find sweet, sharp Mutsus, a cross between the Golden Delicious and the Indo apple, a variety that maintains its shape when cooked.

6 Kingbird Farm chicken eggs
1 cup Crosswinds Creamery milk
8 slices day-old brioche
1 tablespoon butter
maple apples*

1. Whisk together eggs and milk in a baking dish. Add the bread in a single layer, turning until all the egg is absorbed.

2. In a large nonstick skillet, melt butter and saute the soaked bread until golden brown on each side, about 4 minutes.

3. Place two slices of French toast on each of four warmed plates. Top each with a heaping spoonful of the maple-apple mixture.

*For the maple apples:

2 tablespoons butter
2 Littletree Orchards Mutsu apples, peeled and sliced
1 tablespoon water
½ cup Schoolyard Sugarbush maple syrup
pinch of ground cinnamon

1. Heat a large skillet over medium heat. Melt 1 tablespoon butter and add apples, stirring to coat until they begin to caramelize.

2. Add the water, cooking until water has evaporated and apples are tender, about 4 to 5 minutes.

3. Stir in the maple syrup and cinnamon. Remove from heat and set aside.

Pan-Roasted Cauliflower Steaks with Carrot Top Gremolata

MAKES 4 SERVINGS

Eat your cauliflower! The cruciferous vegetable is naturally high in fiber and vitamins and has many health benefits, such as aiding digestion and circulation, strengthening bones, and preventing cancer.

Heavy, large white heads of Denali cauliflower, harvested at Nook & Cranny Farm in Caroline, yield dense, six- to seven-inch, dome-shaped heads with tender, creamy-white florets and superb mild, nutty-sweet flavors. This dish introduces mild-tasting cauliflower to the lively flavors of a gremolata made from spicy garlic and those leafy green carrot tops you didn't know what to do with.

2 heads Nook & Cranny Farm Denali cauliflower
¼ cup extra-virgin olive oil
1 teaspoon onion powder
1 teaspoon cumin powder
kosher salt
freshly ground black pepper
carrot top gremolata*

1. Slice cauliflower heads lengthwise through the core into halves. Cut each half into two steaks approximately 2 inches in width.

2. Preheat oven to 400 degrees F. Arrange the cauliflower steaks on a sheet pan and set aside.

3. In a small bowl, whisk together the olive oil, onion powder, cumin powder, and salt and pepper to taste.

4. Using a pastry brush, coat the cauliflower steaks with the seasoned oil. Transfer the sheet pan to the oven and bake for 10 minutes.

5. Flip the cauliflower over, brush with seasoned oil, and bake for about 10 minutes or until fork-tender and golden brown.

6. Divide cauliflower steaks among 4 warmed plates. Top each steak with a heaping spoonful of gremolata.

*For the carrot top gremolata:

1 cup carrot greens, washed thoroughly and finely chopped
2 cloves Six Circles Farm Spanish Roja garlic, minced
2 teaspoons lemon zest
sea salt
freshly ground black pepper

1. Add the carrot greens, garlic, and lemon zest to a small bowl and stir to combine.

2. Season with salt and pepper to taste.

"Pumpkin Pie" Pancakes with Cinnamon Butter

MAKES 8 SERVINGS

"I would rather sit on a pumpkin, and have it all to myself, than be crowded on a velvet cushion," writes Henry David Thoreau.

An earthy, sweet pumpkin from Mandeville Farm becomes the star of these delicious pancakes that include many of the same ingredients as pumpkin pie, the quintessential fall treat. Like pie, pancakes made from fresh, local pumpkins taste so much better than canned puree from who knows where. The recipe yields eight servings—if you're restrained.

1¼ cups unbleached all-purpose flour
2 tablespoons sugar
2 teaspoons baking powder
½ teaspoon kosher salt
½ teaspoon cinnamon
½ teaspoon ground ginger
pinch of nutmeg
pinch of ground cloves
1 cup Crosswinds Creamery milk
6 tablespoons pumpkin puree*
2 tablespoons butter, melted, plus
    more for skillet
1 Kingbird Farm chicken egg
cinnamon butter**

1. Whisk flour, sugar, baking powder, salt, and spices in a bowl.

2. In a separate bowl, stir together milk, pumpkin puree, butter, and egg. Fold mixture into dry ingredients.

3. Melt butter in a skillet over medium heat; pour 3 to 4 tablespoons of batter for each pancake. Cook pancakes until batter is set and bubbles form on top. Flip and cook until golden brown on both sides.

4. Pile pancakes high on a warm serving platter. Pass family style around the table. Serve with cinnamon butter.

*For the pumpkin puree:

1 Mandeville Farm pumpkin, 4 to 6 pounds
kosher salt

1. Heat oven to 400 degrees F.

2. Cut pumpkin from stem to bottom end and separate each half. Scoop out the seeds and stringy bits.

3. Lightly season inside the pumpkin halves with salt then place cut-side down onto the baking sheet. Bake until the pumpkin is easily pierced with a knife, about 45 minutes to 1 hour. Remove from the oven and allow to cool.

4. Scoop out the soft flesh and place in a food processor. Process until very smooth, 3 to 5 minutes.

**For the cinnamon butter:

4 tablespoons unsalted butter, softened
2 teaspoons ground cinnamon
1 tablespoon powdered sugar

1. In a small bowl, combine softened butter, cinnamon, and sugar. Blend thoroughly.

2. Chill in the fridge until ready to use.

Ziti con Broccoli

MAKES 4 SERVINGS

Hot summer sun can make broccoli tough and bitter, according to Mary McGarry-Newman of Buried Treasures Organic Farm, and fall broccoli is better suited to the early cold and late heat of its growing season. Mary is continually experimenting with varieties to get the best-tasting, best-growing broccoli from the Groton farm to the market and onto your dinner table in this traditional Italian dish.

6 cups Buried Treasures Organic Farm broccoli florets
12 ounces ziti pasta
kosher salt
2 tablespoons salted butter
1 clove Six Circles Farm German Red garlic, crushed
⅔ cup roughly crumbled gorgonzola
pine nuts, toasted until golden
freshly ground black pepper

1. Blanch the broccoli in plenty of boiling water for 3 minutes or so. Drain in a colander and refresh under ice-cold water to preserve its color. Drain again and roughly chop.

2. Cook the pasta in boiling salted water, according to the package instructions, until al dente.

3. Meanwhile, place the butter and garlic into a large frying pan over medium heat and cook for a minute or so, until the garlic is fragrant but not browned. Add the broccoli and cook for 2 to 3 minutes. Stir in the gorgonzola to form a sauce. Season with salt and pepper to taste.

4. Drain the pasta and add to the broccoli mixture and mix well.

5. To serve, divide among 4 warmed bowls and scatter pine nuts over the top of each.

Zuppa Toscana with Cannellini Beans

MAKES 4 TO 6 SERVINGS

This hearty, autumn harvest soup can be traced to hilltop villages in Tuscany where, during the Middle Ages, peasants saved leftover bread crusts and bits of vegetables from the tables of their feudal lords and added them to their own soups and stews at home.

Cannellini beans add earthy and nutty flavor to a comforting and hearty seasonal soup.

2 tablespoons extra-virgin olive oil, plus extra for drizzling
1 medium Valley View Farm Candy onion, diced
2 Humble Hill Farm carrots, peeled and thinly sliced
4 cloves Six Circles Farm Spanish Roja garlic, minced
1 Nook & Cranny Farm Safari zucchini, peeled and thinly sliced
1 Stick and Stone Farm heirloom tomato, diced
1 handful parsley, chopped
1 bunch West Haven Farm Tuscan kale, roughly chopped
1 (15-ounce) can cannellini beans, drained
1 quart vegetable stock
kosher salt
freshly ground black pepper
½ loaf Wide Awake Bakery pain au levain, cut into cubes

1. Heat the oil in a heavy large pot over medium heat. Add the onion, carrots, and garlic. Cook over low heat, about 10 minutes. Add zucchini, tomato, and parsley and cook for 2 more minutes.

2. Add kale, beans, and vegetable stock. Bring to a boil, then reduce heat and simmer for about 30 minutes. Season with salt and pepper to taste.

3. Ladle into individual warmed bowls, ensuring each bowl has a good balance of vegetables and liquid. Arrange bread cubes in each and top with a drizzle of olive oil.

DESSERT

Jonagold Honey-Baked Apples with Maple Whipped Cream

MAKES 4 SERVINGS

It's said that when apples ripen in the fall, we realize what the trees have been up to all summer. At Littletree Orchards in Newfield, nearly ten thousand trees of twenty different apple varieties have produced locally grown fruit for the market since 1975. Tangy and sweet with honeylike flavor notes, Jonagold apples, a cross between the blush-crimson Jonathan and crisp Golden Delicious, are firm enough to hold their own during the cooking process. Baking concentrates the flavors and yields an intensely pure dessert.

Basswood honey is obtained from the blossoms of the basswood tree, sometimes called the "bee tree," since its yellowish-white flowers that drip with fragrant nectar attract honeybees from miles around. It has a deeper, darker color with a full and richer flavor, perfect for this fall comfort-food dessert.

4 Littletree Orchards Jonagold apples

pinch of ground cinnamon for each apple

2 teaspoons Waid's Apiaries basswood honey for each apple

1 teaspoon chopped walnuts for each apple

maple whipped cream*

1. Wash and core each apple, hollowing out the inside while leaving the bottom intact.

2. Place apples in a baking dish coated with nonstick cooking spray.

3. Sprinkle the cavity of each apple with cinnamon; fill each with 2 teaspoons honey and 1 teaspoon chopped walnuts.

4. Cover baking dish with foil. Bake at 350 degrees F until apples are tender, about 1 to 1½ hours. Remove from heat.

5. Transfer each apple to a warmed dessert plate. Top each with a generous dollop of maple whipped cream.

*For the maple whipped cream:

1 cup heavy cream

2 tablespoons Schoolyard Sugarbush maple syrup

½ teaspoon vanilla extract

⅛ teaspoon salt

1. Chill mixing bowl and whisk attachment in the freezer for 10 minutes.

2. Place the cream, maple syrup, vanilla, and salt in the bowl. Beat on medium-high speed until thickened and soft peaks form, about 3 to 5 minutes. Periodically scrape down the sides of the bowl.

Makes 2 cups

ITHACA FARMERS MARKET HISTORY: 1996

In his whimsical children's book *Rootabaga Stories*, author Carl Sandburg writes, "Welcome to rootabaga country, where the railroad tracks go from straight to zig-zag." Ithaca has become "rootabaga" country.

Snow-Covered Last Day of the Season, Let the Games Begin!

It all started on a bone-chilling Saturday, the last day of the market season in 1996. The handful of obstinate vendors, attired in winter habiliments and huddled together against blasts of wind off the lake, waited for folks they called the "hell-or-high-water shoppers." Perhaps it is the cold that turns a person giddy. Maybe it was the market's near-empty wooden planks that beckoned. But Steve Sierigk had a twinkle in his eye. A greeting card vendor and unapologetic prankster, he suggested combining the winter sport of curling with the market's winter crops. And after the first vegetable came rolling down the center of the pavilion like a primitive bowling ball, that day—and each ensuing final day of the season, typically the third weekend in December—would never be the same.

By the following year, Steve began to codify rules, creating a jovial competition of root vegetable marksmanship. He designed the court, enlisted Blue Heron Farm to bring extra rutabagas, and became "commissioner" of the contest. There were early attempts to include other

Rutabaga Alley, Fling That Thing!

Contestant Launches Root Vegetable

projectiles, but he restricted everything except that bulbous cross between cabbage and turnip.

Contestants were encouraged by cheering crowds as they pitched numbered rutabagas toward a parking cone seventy-nine feet away. Once a rutabaga was tossed, it remained on the field of play until other contestants rolled, subject to being knocked by subsequent rolls. The contestant whose vegetable remained closest to the target was declared the winner. National Public Radio compared the event to a cross between bowling and shuffleboard.

The day now begins with a parade of "athletes" led by the rutabaga god and goddess carrying flaming torches, and the crowd is serenaded by the cruciferous chorus singing the rutabaga curl song. Root, root, root for the rutabaga!

Winners, from typically more than one hundred competitors, receive medals. Steve Paisley, a first-time curler, won a silver medal in 2009.

Determined to improve his performance, the following year Paisley froze his rutabaga, expecting an advantage, but it exploded on impact with his first throw. The next year, a new rule was put into place dictating that all contestants use fresh rutabagas for the competition.

In 2002, the youngest-ever contestant, eight-year-old David Tregaskis, took the gold medal. To date, no champion has ever successfully defended his or her title, although in 2008, local attorney Ray Schlather became the first curler to medal twice, taking the silver after a similar performance in 2006.

Although Steve retired as commissioner in 2011, his legacy is the International Rutabaga Curling Championship, turning a sparse sales day into a festive event that evolved into what can only be described as community theater.

"Do anything," writes Walt Whitman, "but let it produce joy."

WINTER

Winter is the time for comfort,
for good food and warmth.

—Edith Sitwell

BEVERAGES AND COCKTAILS

Ginger Greens Tea

MAKES 4 SERVINGS

Soothing, immune-boosting ginger tea is best known as a winter drink during cold and flu season. However, drinking ginger tea is lovely at any time of the year, providing a morning or afternoon pick-me-up.

Humble Hill Farm brings baby ginger to the market with the aromatic leaves and stalks still attached. The greens, infused with the same ginger flavor, are used to make this invigorating tea.

Goldenrod is a favorite of the honeybee, and it creates a very dark and distinct honey, tasting similar to butterscotch.

1 quart water

squeezed juice of 1 lemon

¼ cup chopped Humble Hill Farm baby ginger leaves

¼ cup Bright Raven Apiary goldenrod honey

1. Bring the water to a boil in a saucepan. Add lemon juice and ginger leaves to the water. Remove from heat. Steep for 20 minutes.

2. Whisk in the honey. Strain the sweetened tea into a pitcher.

3. Refrigerate until ready to use. Serve hot or iced.

"Old Wives' Tale" Hot Toddy

MAKES 1 DRINK

Some folks claim a hot toddy relieves symptoms of the common cold or flu, but think of this drink as a warming pick-me-up any time of the day or night during the cold winter months.

Honey bees visit a wide variety of flowering plants to obtain nectar and pollen as food for themselves and their colony. The dark, monofloral Japanese knotweed honey from Bright Raven Apiary is a rich source of therapeutic, immune-boosting plant compounds.

1 tablespoon Bright Raven Apiary
   Japanese knotweed raw honey
1 ounce whiskey
¼ ounce fresh lemon juice
1 heaping teaspoon black tea leaves
1 cup water
lemon wheel, thinly sliced

1. Coat the bottom of a handled mug with honey. Add the whiskey and lemon juice.

2. Add tea leaves to a teapot. In a small pan, bring water to a boil, pour into the teapot, and allow to steep for about 3 to 5 minutes but no longer.

3. Pour the steaming tea into the mug and stir.

4. Float the lemon wheel on the surface of the drink. Serve immediately.

Sweater Weather

MAKES 1 DRINK

Normal winter low temperatures in Ithaca drop to a bone-chilling 15 degrees with occasional dips below zero. Shake off the cold-weather chill with this maple syrup–spiked cocktail meant to convey the feeling your favorite winter sweater brings about when you first put it on for the season. The dark, robust flavor of maple syrup from Schoolyard Sugarbush in nearby Newfield contrasts with the bourbon and brightness of the orange bitters to make a refreshing and comforting cold-weather cocktail, warming your soul from the inside out.

1½ ounces bourbon
¾ ounce lemon juice
¾ ounce orange juice
¾ ounce Schoolyard Sugarbush
  maple syrup
2 or 3 dashes orange bitters

1. Combine bourbon, lemon juice, orange juice, and maple syrup in a mixing glass filled with cracked ice. Shake vigorously.

2. Strain into a lowball glass. Dash bitters over top.

Warm Woolly Sheep

MAKES 1 DRINK

The bedtime ritual of drinking a glass of warm milk has been passed down through generations as a way of melting away the stresses of the day before entering slumber. And there is both wisdom and tradition in spiking the warm liquid to signal the brain that it's time to sleep. The addition of scotch and scotch-based Drambuie to warm the local "grassmilk" starts out silky smooth and slightly smoky, then adds layers of soft, dessert-like sweetness before a blend of spices envelops the tongue. Comforting, pleasing, and calming, it lingers in dreams until morning.

6 ounces Crosswinds Creamery milk
1 ounce scotch
¼ ounce Drambuie
1 dash Angostura bitters

1. Heat milk in a small saucepan over medium heat until just beginning to bubble.

2. Stir in scotch and Drambuie, then pour into a warm mug.

3. Dash bitters over top.

SALADS AND SMALL PLATES

"Aglio e Olio" Mashed Potatoes

MAKES 4 TO 6 SERVINGS

According to British writer A. A. Milne, "If a fellow really likes potatoes, he must be a pretty decent sort of fellow." Richard Sabol is that sort of fellow, offering as many as fifteen well-grown potato varieties at his market stand. Notable among the tasty tubers, Keuka Gold is a handsome, gold-fleshed potato, the Cornell breeding program's answer to Yukon Gold.

Spanish Roja translates to Spanish red garlic, a favorite of garlic connoisseurs and chefs, sought after for its plump bulbs, robust flavor, and easy-to-peel quality.

2 pounds Sabol's Farm Keuka Gold potatoes, peeled and cut into 1-inch chunks

8 Six Circles Farm Spanish Roja garlic cloves, peeled

1 teaspoon kosher salt

¼ cup extra-virgin olive oil

1. Bring a large pot of water to a boil. Add potatoes, garlic, and salt. Reduce heat and simmer until potatoes are tender, about 15 minutes.

2. Drain potatoes and garlic, reserving ¼ cup of cooking liquid. Mash together potatoes and garlic. Beat in olive oil and thin to desired consistency with reserved cooking liquid.

3. Transfer to a warmed serving bowl and pass family style around the table.

Baby Ginger Rice

MAKES 4 SERVINGS

At Humble Hill Farm, beautiful pink-and-cream-colored baby ginger is harvested in late September to early October. Less time in the ground results in a more citrusy, floral flavor and less fibrous flesh. Whereas mature ginger has a tough skin and is very potent, baby ginger is tender and mild.

Ginger rice is versatile and a perfect pairing for Asian- and Indian-inspired meals like curries and stir-fries or meat or vegetable main dishes.

1 tablespoon butter
2 tablespoons minced Humble Hill
    Farm baby ginger
1 clove Six Circles Farm Spanish Roja
    garlic, minced
1½ cups chicken or vegetable stock
1 cup basmati rice
1 teaspoon sea salt
green onions, chopped into chiffonade

1. Melt the butter in a medium-sized pot over medium heat. Add ginger and garlic and cook, about 30 seconds.

2. Add the stock, rice, and salt to the pot and bring it to a boil. Reduce heat and cook, about 12 minutes, stirring frequently. Remove from heat and let rest, about 10 minutes.

3. Transfer to a warmed serving bowl, scatter green onions over top, and pass family style around the table.

Bacon-Apple-Kale Sandwich

MAKES 2 SANDWICHES

The BLT is universal, but there's really only one best time to enjoy a bacon, lettuce, and tomato sandwich—in the height of summer when tomatoes are plentiful. A fleeting joy, the out-of-season BLT is replaced with the BAK, a bacon, apple, and kale sandwich during winter months. It's a surprisingly awesome alternative, especially if you use all market ingredients.

6 slices Glenwood Farms bison bacon
4 slices Wide Awake Bakery
   sourdough bread
1 handful Nook & Cranny curly kale,
   stems removed, chopped into
   confetti
1 Littletree Orchards Ida Red apple,
   thinly sliced
1 tablespoon mayonnaise

1. In a heavy skillet, cook the bacon to desired crispness. Transfer to a paper towel to drain.

2. Toast the bread in a toaster or under the broiler.

3. To assemble sandwiches, evenly divide the kale between two slices of bread. Layer each with apple and bacon. Spread mayonnaise on remaining slices and flip over to make sandwiches. Slice sandwiches in half. Serve immediately.

Bourbon Glazed Carrots

MAKES 6 SERVINGS

At Humble Hill Farm, once garlic is harvested, Rick and Courtney rework the land and put in carrots for the winter. After a few light frosts, bugs have died down, there's more rain and moisture, and carrot roots become even sweeter, which explains why true winter-harvested carrots are a delicacy.

The smooth flavor of bourbon, with notes of oak, vanilla, and caramel, pairs perfectly with the earthy sweetness of the deep orange French Bolero carrots. The spirit's flavor profile is a distinct component of the finished dish.

1 stick unsalted butter
2 pounds Humble Hill Farm French
   Bolero carrots, peeled, cut into
   equal-sized pieces
½ cup bourbon
⅓ cup brown sugar
thyme leaves, chopped into chiffonade

1. Melt butter in a heavy skillet over medium-high heat. When butter begins to foam, add carrots. Cook, stirring frequently, until carrots begin to brown around the edges, about 5 to 6 minutes.

2. Reduce heat to medium-low. Add the bourbon. Cook, stirring frequently, until bourbon is nearly evaporated, about 2 minutes.

3. Sprinkle in brown sugar. Stir until carrots are almost cooked through, about 5 to 6 minutes. When carrots are nearly tender, raise heat to medium-high to thicken the glaze, about 30 seconds. Remove from heat.

4. Transfer to a warmed serving dish, scatter thyme over top, and pass family style around the table.

"Championship" Rutabaga Soup with Bacon

MAKES 6 SERVINGS

Rutabagas become sweet as temperatures drop and are at their very best during winter. The name is derived from the Swedish word rotabagga, *meaning "round root."*

Goodness gracious, great balls of rutabaga! Once a passed-over vegetable, the rutabaga has become something of a celebrity at the market. Ever since 1996, vendors have ended the season with a competition that involves rolling the root vegetable down the center of the pavilion. Because of its rounded shape, only rutabagas are allowed in what is now known as the International Rutabaga Curling Championship.

2 tablespoons unsalted butter

1 medium Valley View Farm Candy onion, diced

1 medium Sabol's Farm rutabaga, peeled and diced

2 cloves Six Circles Farm Spanish Roja garlic, thinly sliced

1 cup heavy cream

1 cup Crosswinds Creamery milk

3½ cups vegetable stock

3 tablespoons Schoolyard Sugarbush maple syrup

sea salt

freshly ground black pepper

3 slices Glenwood Farms bison bacon, diced

1. Melt butter in a large saucepan over low heat. Add onion and cook, about 3 to 4 minutes. Add rutabaga and garlic and cook until rutabaga can be pierced with a knife, about 15 to 20 minutes.

2. Separately in a 3-quart saucepan, bring cream, milk, and stock to a simmer.

3. Add cream mixture to the rutabaga saucepan, stir in maple syrup, and simmer for another 10 or 15 minutes. Puree in a blender and return to a clean saucepan. Season with salt and pepper to taste.

4. Cook bacon in a small skillet until lightly browned. Remove from heat and drain on a paper towel.

5. Reheat soup, and ladle into 6 warmed bowls. Scatter bacon over each serving.

Deviled Duck Eggs

MAKES 1 DOZEN HALVES

A classic cocktail party dish, deviled eggs are halved hard-boiled eggs whose yolks are scooped out, mashed together with mayonnaise, mustard, and a dash of Tabasco, spooned back into each egg white half, and finished with a festive sprinkle of paprika.

Duck eggs are richer and more flavorful than chicken eggs, with large yolks that remain creamy and moist once hard boiled, perfect for deviled eggs, in which the yolks are, of course, the star of the dish.

6 Jasper Meadows Farm duck eggs
3 tablespoons mayonnaise
1 teaspoon Dijon mustard
1 tablespoon chopped chives
2 dashes Tabasco sauce
kosher salt
freshly ground black pepper
smoked Spanish paprika

1. Fill a large pot with 2 inches of water and bring to a boil. Place eggs in the water, cover and cook, about 8 minutes. When the eggs are done, transfer to an ice bath and cool completely.

2. In a small bowl, stir together the mayonnaise, mustard, and chives. Season with Tabasco and salt and pepper to taste. Set aside.

3. Crack eggshells and peel in the ice bath.

4. On a cutting board, halve the eggs and carefully remove yolks. Mash yolks with the mayo-mustard mix and stir to combine.

5. Spoon egg yolk mixture into the egg white halves. Sprinkle each with paprika. To serve, arrange filled eggs on a serving platter.

"Heaven and Earth"

In German it's called himmelund erde, *which means heaven and earth. You reach up to heaven to pick apples, whereas turnips and potatoes are pulled from the earth. All three ingredients appear at the market around the same time, so this dish is truly an expression of the season. Sprinkle with cinnamon to add warm, spicy flavors, and to honor tradition, serve with sauerkraut and sausage.*

3 Sabol's Farm Keuka Gold potatoes, quartered
2 small Fort Baptist Farm turnips, halved
2 medium Littletree Orchards Northern Spy apples, cored, peeled, and quartered
1 tablespoon butter
splash of Crosswinds Creamery milk
kosher salt
freshly ground black pepper
ground cinnamon

1. Boil potatoes and turnips in water until about ¾ done. Add the apples and boil until all ingredients are soft. Drain.

2. With a hand masher or blender, blend with butter and milk until smooth. Season with salt and pepper to taste.

3. Transfer to a warmed serving dish, sprinkle cinnamon over top, and pass family style around the table.

Herb-Roasted Celery Root

MAKES 4 SERVINGS

Hunt for these at the market. Also known as celeriac, these sometimes-overlooked root vegetables are round, knobby, and about the size of a grapefruit. Despite the name, they're actually not the root of celery stalks, but rather bred specifically for the root instead of the stalks.

The best way to bring out celery root's slightly sweet and nutty flavor is by roasting. Fresh herbs add bright notes and essential micronutrients to this side dish.

1 large Stick and Stone Farm celery root
2 tablespoons olive oil
¼ teaspoon dried basil
¼ teaspoon dried oregano
¼ teaspoon dried thyme
¼ teaspoon red pepper flakes
parsley, chopped into chiffonade

1. Preheat oven to 400 degrees F.

2. Peel the celery root until all the brown peel is gone. Chop into ½-inch chunks.

3. Add the chunks to a bowl with olive oil, basil, oregano, thyme, and pepper flakes. Toss to coat.

4. On a sheet pan, spread into a single layer. Place in the oven and roast for 20 to 25 minutes or until golden on the outside and soft inside. Remove from oven.

5. Transfer to a warmed serving plate, scatter parsley over top, and pass family style around the table.

Roasted "Bull's Blood" Beets with Apple Cider Vinaigrette

MAKES 4 SERVINGS

John Reynolds and Shannon O'Connor of Daring Drake Farm are sixteen-year veterans at the market, arriving each week with a variety of fruits from the orchard and eggs from the farm's flock of ducks. In Native American culture, the black duck symbolizes adaptability and resourcefulness, and with the eighty varieties of apples grown on two orchards three miles apart in Ovid, the resourceful couple launched Blackduck Cidery. For this recipe, John suggests Banker's Blend cider (named for Ovid's historic John Banker Farm), a tannic English-style cider, along with his raw, unfiltered apple cider vinegar.

Those brilliant red burgundy beets at the Shagbark Gardens stand are an heirloom variety called Bull's Blood, sweet and nutty when roasted. Sliced open, the globe-shaped roots have deep red and white concentric rings. Save the plant's dark, great-tasting leaves for salad mixes or blanch like spinach.

6 medium Shagbark Gardens Bull's Blood beets

2 tablespoons Blackduck Cidery Banker's Blend apple cider

1 tablespoon Blackduck Cidery apple cider vinegar

1 tablespoon Waid's Apiaries buckwheat honey

1 tablespoon extra-virgin olive oil

kosher salt

freshly ground black pepper

2 teaspoons herbs de Provence

2 ounces Old Chatham Creamery goat cheese

1. Preheat oven to 400 degrees F.

2. Trim greens and stems from beets. Place in a deep baking dish. Cover with foil and bake for 1 hour.

3. Remove dish from oven, keeping it covered, and allow to cool, about 30 minutes. Slip the skin off each beet and cut into wedges.

4. Whisk cider, cider vinegar, honey, and oil in a mixing bowl. Add the beets, season with salt and pepper to taste, and toss with herbs de Provence.

5. Transfer to a serving plate, top with goat cheese dollops, and pass family style around the table.

Sauteed Russian Kale with Peperoncino

MAKES 4 SERVINGS

Leafy green kale can be found year-round but thrives in cold weather, and it's also one of the most nutrient-dense veggies at the market. This healthy side dish is an excellent source of both fiber and calcium and boasts impressive amounts of vitamins K, A, B6, and C.

Heirloom Russian kales produce more vibrantly colored leaves as the temperature drops. Red and white varieties are similar in taste and appearance; however, Red Russian kale has purple veins whereas the veins of White Russian are white.

1 bunch Main Street Farm Red Russian kale
1 bunch Fort Baptist Farm White Russian kale
2 tablespoons extra-virgin olive oil
2 cloves Six Circles Farm Spanish Roja garlic, thinly sliced
pinch of red pepper flakes (peperoncino)
sea salt
freshly ground black pepper

1. Pull the kale leaves from their stems and tear into pieces.

2. Combine oil, garlic, and red pepper flakes in a large saute pan over medium heat. Saute for 1 to 2 minutes. Add the kale leaves, season with salt and pepper to taste, and toss to coat. Saute for 4 to 5 minutes on medium heat, stirring often. Remove from heat.

3. Transfer to a warmed serving plate and pass family style around the table.

Winter Borscht Salad

MAKES 4 TO 6 SERVINGS

"The beet is the most intense of vegetables," writes Tom Robbins. "Beets are deadly serious."

Beet soup is most associated with Russian and Polish cuisines, although it actually originated in Ukraine, dating back to the fourteenth century, where it was eaten mostly by the peasantry. Borscht, meaning "sour soup," has become a cooking classic in a multitude of versions and interpretations, including a serious, market-inspired salad with many of the soup's traditional ingredients.

1 pound Shagbark Gardens Bull's Blood beets
1 garlic clove, minced
2 teaspoons Dijon mustard
¼ cup sour cream
1 teaspoon fresh lemon juice
1 tablespoon chopped dill
1 medium head Nook & Cranny Farm Space cabbage, shredded
1 hard-boiled Kingbird Farm chicken egg, chopped

1. Peel and grate the raw beets.

2. Combine garlic, mustard, sour cream, lemon juice, and dill in a mixing bowl.

3. Add shredded cabbage and grated beets. Toss to coat.

4. Transfer to a chilled serving plate. Scatter chopped egg over top. Pass family style around the table.

MAIN DISHES

Mixed Root Vegetable Hash

MAKES 4 SERVINGS

In the words of poet and teacher Rumi, "Don't think the garden loses its ecstasy in Winter. It's quiet, but the roots are down there riotous."

Winter vegetables are harvested when temperatures begin to drop, and one thing they all have in common is that they just taste better in the wintertime. This is a clean-out-the-fridge sort of hash, a combination of nutritious root vegetables, versatile, satisfying, and prepared in less than thirty minutes in one pan.

1 tablespoon olive oil
1 cup of diced Valley View Farm
    Candy onion
2 cloves Six Circles Farm German
    Red garlic, chopped
2 cups of diced Sabol's Farm Keuka
    Gold potato
½ cup of diced Shagbark Gardens
    Bull's Blood beet
½ cup of diced Jackman Vineyards
    sweet potato
½ cup of diced Nook & Cranny Farm
    parsnip
½ cup of diced Humble Hill Farm
    carrot
kosher salt
freshly ground black pepper
parsley, chopped into chiffonade

1. Heat a large skillet on medium heat and add 1 tablespoon of oil. Add onion and garlic and saute until onions begin to soften, about 2 to 3 minutes.

2. Add potatoes, beets, sweet potatoes, parsnips, and carrots to the skillet and cook on medium heat, about 10 to 15 minutes, stirring frequently, until veggies are cooked through. Remove from heat. Season with salt and pepper to taste.

3. Transfer to a warmed serving dish, scatter parsley over top, and pass family style around the table.

Parsnips, Bistro-Style

MAKES 6 SERVINGS

Once parsnips are kissed by frost, they become sweeter and tastier, traditionally harvested in winter. This smashed (écrasé) version is popular on Paris bistro menus, a pleasantly rustic variation with peppery and earthy notes and a hint of spice. Finish with flecks of deep green parsley as a flavor booster.

2 pounds Nook & Cranny Farm parsnips, peeled, cut into 2-inch pieces
2 cups chicken broth
1¼ cups water
¼ cup Crosswinds Creamery milk
1 tablespoon butter
½ teaspoon sea salt
¼ teaspoon freshly ground black pepper
parsley, chopped into chiffonade

1. In a medium saucepan, bring parsnips, chicken broth, and water to a boil. Reduce heat and simmer, about 25 to 30 minutes, until parsnips are very tender. Drain.

2. Add parsnips to a food processor with milk, butter, salt, and pepper. Process until smooth.

3. Ladle into each of 6 warmed bowls. Scatter parsley over each serving.

Vegetable Pot-au-Feu

MAKES 6 SERVINGS

Fill your market basket with the makings of this winter vegetable interpretation of the French national dish, translated as "pot on the fire." As its name suggests, in medieval France, peasant households had a single hearth in which a small fire burned for most of the day. Ingredients were thrown into a large earthenware pot suspended from a hook, covered with water, and left to cook slowly for several hours.

2 large Humble Hill Farm French Bolero carrots, peeled, cut into 2-inch lengths

3 small Humble Hill Farm Bulgarian Giant leeks, white part only, cut into 2-inch lengths

2 medium Nook & Cranny Farm parsnips, peeled, cut into 2-inch lengths

3 small Fort Baptist Farm turnips, peeled and halved

2 medium Valley View Farm Candy onions, peeled

5 cups vegetable stock

kosher salt

freshly ground black pepper

parsley, chopped into chiffonade

1. Place carrots, leeks, parsnips, turnips, onions, and stock in a large pot and bring to a boil. Reduce heat and simmer until vegetables are tender, about 20 to 25 minutes. Remove from heat. Season with salt and pepper to taste.

2. To serve, ladle into each of 4 warmed bowls. Scatter parsley over each serving.

DESSERT

Musician's Dessert

MAKES 4 TO 6 SERVINGS

The postre de músico *is a traditional dessert in the Catalonia region of northeastern Spain, adopted from the early practice of feeding strolling musicians who didn't have the opportunity to enjoy a whole meal. Served after dinner with dessert wines, it is meant to be nibbled and sipped while lingering at the table with good company.*

Autumn Stoscheck joined the market in 2002 when Eve's Cidery was a start-up enterprise. Since then, Eve's has become one of the nation's most influential cideries, elevating the crafting of organic cider into an art form. To accompany the Catalan-inspired dessert plate, Eve's Cidery Essence is a lush, concentrated ice cider made from wild-harvested apples.

1 handful Sabol's Farm walnuts, shelled
1 handful almonds, shelled
1 handful pine nuts
1 handful dried figs
1 handful dried apricots
1 handful dried dates
1 wedge Snow Farm Creamery Gouda
   cheese

1. To serve, place cheese at the center of a party platter and arrange the nuts and fruits separately according to variety, allowing guests to assemble their own mixture.

ITHACA FARMERS MARKET HISTORY: TESTIMONIALS

In the early days, there was a real sense of camaraderie and family among the vendors and mostly local customers. The ethos of 'make it, bake it, grow it yourself' and the clarity of the thirty-mile radius was a real unifying force at that time.

—Anna Steinkraus, Littletree Orchards, member since 1973. President of the board from 1983 to 1994, Anna was pivotal in the negotiations with the city for a permanent location and the building of the pavilion itself. Her daughter Amara, who now often works at the market stand, was born mere hours after the city council meeting at which Anna signed the twenty-year lease for Steamboat Landing.

Ithaca has a tendency to be very community oriented. There is a very strong community sense here, and that is demonstrated in the market as well. Part of it is the pavilion itself, built by the membership. Members were tired of putting up pop-up tents in the parking lot. The structure we built has been copied all over the country. There's one in California that looks just like ours, except it's surrounded by palm trees.

—Wendy and Andy Ives, Ithaca Soap, members since 2001

Steamboat Landing before the Pavilion, 1986

When I first started here, we were begging people to come, and we could barely fill the market. Now there are people on waiting lists, wanting to sell their products here. We have local folks who we see every week, and we have tourists during June, July, and August. It's so great for people who come up with entrepreneurial ideas, who create something, to be able to support the community and themselves.

—Peggy Aker, Macro-Mama, member since 1992

I think people really appreciate meeting the person who grows the food or makes the product. Because I can answer any of their questions, it's important to me and to my buyers. What we do here is so personal. I feel a real connection to all my work, and when someone else appreciates it enough to take it home, it's just a very good feeling.

—David Kingsbury, Earth 'n' Fire Pottery, member since 1978

As a wood carver and painter, I'm called a folk artist, and I call the market my "summer studio." Time spent there is important to getting my work seen. It's like a craft fair every weekend only two miles from my home. Once people hear me tapping away, they understand my work in a more visceral way. I find it energizing to hear people's reactions to my work and to answer the questions of budding woodcarvers. I'm truly happy to have an alternative to the gallery scene.

—Mary Shelley, Art by Mary Shelley, member since 1977

There has always been a significant element of tourism at the market, because of the people coming back to Ithaca or a family visiting someone going to school here. It brings not only national but international visitors passing through town, and when you come here, the people you know and love want to show you their favorite things to do and places to go. Over the years, the market has become that local tradition.

—Jan Norman, Silk Oak, member since 1996

Robin Ostfeld, Summer Bounty at Blue Heron Farm, 1994

Hangar Theatre "Kidstuff" Performance, 1990

In the turmoil created by the Vietnam War, our country of Cambodia fell into the hands of the Khmer Rouge, who enslaved the country and killed many people. We were fortunate to escape to neighboring Thailand, where we cooked food for fellow refugees at the UN camp after crossing the border. With the help of an American refugee program and financial assistance from the local First Baptist Church, we came to Ithaca in 1979 and were accepted as market vendors in 2002, preparing a dozen different offerings of traditional Cambodian dishes.

—Bong and Mum Sen, Khmer Angkor, members since 2002

My husband Chris and I were among the very first vendors, not the first day, but within a week or two. We sold our wood crafts from an old navy table set up behind our truck, no cover, so when it rained, we got soaked. A young woman who used to ride her bicycle to the market now comes with her daughter and grandchildren, so we've served three generations of that family. The local rule was in effect from day one, so early on, when we discovered a vendor who was buying his produce at the Syracuse market and selling it here, we threw him out.

—Ginny Gartlein, Raintree Farm, member since 1973

Fiddler at the Market, Taughannock Boulevard, 1986

YEAR ROUND

A recipe is only a theme, which an intelligent cook can play each time with a variation.

—Madame Benoit

BEVERAGES AND COCKTAILS

Apple Cider "Snakebite"

MAKES 1 DRINK

The Snakebite is a British pub mainstay, fashioned with crisp, dry hard cider, then accented with a layer of dark and creamy beer. It's a refreshing shandy-style sipper the Brits often serve with a side of fried green tomatoes.

In his quest to produce ciders that speak of our specific region, John Reynolds of Blackduck Cidery uses wild native yeasts for fermentation, allowing nature to take its course. His Basque-style, unfiltered and unfined No Pasaran cider provides a worthy partner to a deep, dark, richly flavored stout.

8 ounces Blackduck Cidery No Pasaran cider, chilled
8 ounces stout beer, chilled

1. Wet a 16-ounce beer pint glass with cold water. Place glass in the freezer compartment of a refrigerator for about 30 minutes.

2. Remove from the freezer and fill the glass halfway with the hard cider.

3. Very slowly pour the stout over the back of a wide bar spoon so that the beer doesn't mix, but rests on top of the cider.

Minted "Animal Behavior" Iced Coffee

MAKES 1 DRINK

Mixing micro-lot beans from Colombia and Brazil, Andrew Ballard and Matt Marks of Forty Weight Coffee Roasters created a blend they call Animal Behavior, producing a crisp, round brew with notes of sweet cherry and a refined acidity. Pick up a supply of fresh mint at the market to make an infused syrup that tweaks this iced coffee.

1 cup freshly brewed Forty Weight
   Roasters Animal Behavior coffee
1 tablespoon heavy cream
1 tablespoon mint simple syrup*

1. Combine coffee, cream, and simple syrup in a tall glass filled with ice. Stir to combine.

*For the mint simple syrup:

½ cup granulated sugar
¾ cup fresh mint leaves, chopped
½ cup boiling water

1. Combine the sugar and mint leaves in a heatproof bowl.

2. Add the boiling water and stir until the sugar is dissolved.

3. Steep the mint leaves for 15 minutes.

4. Strain into a jar; cover and refrigerate until ready to use.

Mushroom Mule

MAKES 1 DRINK

In 2009, transplanted New York City couple Joe and Wendy Rizzo landed in Ithaca as mushroom growers, selling gourmet mushrooms at the market every Saturday. A decade later, the Rizzos refined the art of edible fungus at the other end of Cayuga Lake. Their infused vodkas—Hen of the Woods, Enoki, Shiitake, Destroying Angel, Pleurotis, and Spore—showcase the subtle, earthy nuances and umami of each different gourmet mushroom variety in the base spirit.

A mushroom-inspired version of the classic Moscow Mule is spiked with deep, woodsy Hen of the Woods vodka and topped up with ginger beer from the Ithaca Beer Company.

1½ ounces Mushroom Spirits Distillery
  Hen of the Woods vodka
½ ounce lime juice
4 ounces Ithaca Beer Company
  Ginger Beer
lime wheel

1. Fill a Moscow Mule mug (or highball glass) with ice.

2. Add vodka and lime juice. Top up with ginger beer and garnish with lime wheel.

Rosemary's Baby

MAKES 1 DRINK

Since gin is already a characteristically bold spirit, fragrant rosemary is a fitting herbal complement for this cocktail. Choose a juniper-forward gin to meld with rosemary-infused simple syrup, citrus aromatics of fresh lemon, and effervescence of sparkling cider.

Redbyrd Orchard's Workman Dry is made from a blend of more than twenty-five varieties of heirloom, bittersweet, bittersharp, sharp, and wild seedling apples.

1 ounce gin
½ ounce rosemary simple syrup*
1 teaspoon fresh lemon juice
Redbyrd Orchard Workman Dry
　cider, chilled
fresh rosemary sprig

1. In a tall flute, add gin, simple syrup, and lemon juice.

2. Top up with the cider and garnish with rosemary sprig.

*For the rosemary simple syrup:

½ cup sugar
¼ cup ground rosemary (use an herb grinder or coffee
　grinder)
½ cup water

1. Combine ingredients in a small saucepan and bring to a boil. Reduce heat to a simmer, and stir until the sugar dissolves. Remove from heat and allow to steep for 45 minutes.

2. Strain the mixture through a fine mesh strainer into a clean jar. Refrigerate until ready to use.

SALADS AND SMALL PLATES

Cabernet Franc Compound Butter

MAKES 8 TO 10 SERVINGS

Two friends and partners, winemaker Lou Damiani and vineyardist Phil Davis, set out to prove that exceptional red wines could be made in the Finger Lakes. They planted cabernet franc in 1997 and produced the first vintage in 2003. They began bringing fine wines to the market in 2012.

An herbaceous compound butter with the floral, earthy notes of Damiani cabernet franc adds oomph to the blandest of dishes, everything from steak to grilled vegetables, tossed with pasta, or simply spread on a slice of toasted sourdough.

1 cup Damiani Wine Cellars cabernet franc
½ tablespoon fresh rosemary, minced
½ tablespoon fresh chives, minced
½ teaspoon Waid's Apiaries wildflower honey
2 sticks butter, softened to room temperature
kosher salt
freshly ground black pepper
2 tablespoons chives, chopped into chiffonade

1. In a small saucepan, combine wine, rosemary, chives, and honey. Bring to a boil, then reduce heat and simmer until wine has reduced to about 2 tablespoons, about 10 to 12 minutes. Remove from heat and strain the herbs.

2. In a large bowl, combine butter and reduced red wine and season with salt and pepper to taste. Use a hand mixer or spatula to mix until smooth.

3. Fold in chives and transfer mixture to a large piece of plastic wrap. Tightly wrap butter and form into a log. Twist ends of plastic wrap to seal and refrigerate until firm.

4. Slice butter into pats when ready to serve.

Deli Potato Salad

MAKES 4 SERVINGS

As an avid potato grower, Richard Sabol likes to talk about a variety called Nicola. Developed in Germany from a cross between a wild potato variety and Clivia, Nicola potatoes are yellow fleshed with a mild, nutty, and buttery flavor, best-known for retaining their shape once cooked, which makes them ideal for this dressed-in-mayonnaise delicatessen standard.

4 Sabol's Farm Nicola potatoes, peeled and cubed
1 cup mayonnaise
1 teaspoon dried dill
1 teaspoon celery salt
½ teaspoon paprika
¼ cup finely chopped Humble Hill Farm French Bolero carrots
¼ cup finely chopped pimento
3 tablespoons rice vinegar

1. In a large stockpot full of salted water, bring the potatoes to a boil. Cook until tender, about 10 to 15 minutes. Drain and allow to cool.

2. Meanwhile, in a small mixing bowl, combine the mayonnaise, dill, celery salt, paprika, carrots, and pimento. Whisk until smooth.

3. Add potatoes to a large mixing bowl. Drizzle the rice vinegar over the potatoes.

4. Add the mayonnaise mix to the bowl. Fold gently to combine ingredients. Chill in the fridge.

5. Transfer to a serving bowl and pass family style around the table.

Grilled "Goblin" Cheese Sandwich with Dill Mayonnaise

MAKES 1 SANDWICH

According to legendary chef James Beard, "Too few people understand a really good sandwich."

The modern version of the grilled cheese sandwich originated in the 1920s, when inexpensive sliced bread and American cheese became easily available.

Crosswinds Creamery Goblin made its debut at the market on Halloween weekend in 2015. Semi-firm, Alpine-style, and aged for more than three months, the handcrafted cheese has spicy, nutty flavors, with a subtle aroma from the brine aging. This perfectly melting cheese is well-suited to an upgraded grilled cheese sandwich, satisfyingly indulgent with just enough herbal mayonnaise. This well-constructed creation depends on thick slices of sourdough, buttery-browned in a cast-iron skillet.

2 slices Wide Awake Bakery pain au levain
butter
dill mayonnaise*
2 ounces Crosswinds Creamery Goblin cheese, thinly sliced

1. Heat a cast-iron skillet over medium-low heat.

2. Thinly spread one side of each bread slice with butter. Spread the other side of each slice with mayonnaise and place the bread, mayonnaise-side down, in the skillet. Divide the cheese evenly on top of the buttered slices. Adjust the heat so the bread browns gently.

3. When the cheese is about halfway melted, use a spatula to flip one slice over on top of the other. Keep turning the sandwich, each time pressing gently, until both sides are golden brown, and the cheese is melted. Remove from heat.

4. Transfer sandwich to a plate and serve with a pickle.

*For the dill mayonnaise:

¼ teaspoon finely grated lemon zest
squeezed juice of ½ lemon
¼ cup dill, chopped into chiffonade
½ cup mayonnaise
pinch of sea salt

1. In a small bowl, whisk together lemon zest and juice, dill, mayonnaise, and salt.

McSorley's Cheese and Cracker Plate with Beer Chutney

MAKES 1 SERVING

The undisputed champion of New York City drinking institutions is an ancient taproom called McSorley's Old Ale House, founded by John McSorley in 1854. Since then, the bar has welcomed a long list of famous patrons including Teddy Roosevelt, Babe Ruth, Lou Gehrig, Woody Guthrie, Mickey Mantle, and John Lennon. Abraham Lincoln visited after giving his famous Cooper Union address in 1860.

Besides serving house ale, the bar sells a modest, quirky cheese plate with raw white onions, saltine crackers, and a side of mustard. A reimagined, market-inspired plate includes Kaerphilly, Snow Farm Creamery's version of a savory cheese, originally made to feed Welsh coal miners, and a sweet-and-sour chutney in place of onion and mustard.

1 wedge Snow Farm Creamery
   Kaerphilly cheese
1 sleeve saltine crackers
beer chutney*

1. Using a sharp, thin knife, slice the cheese in neat tablets slightly smaller than the saltines.

2. Arrange the cheese and crackers on a serving platter. Serve with a ramekin of chutney.

*For the beer chutney:

3 Littletree Orchards Empire apples, peeled, cored, and cut into ½-inch pieces
1 cup raisins
½ medium Valley View Farm Candy onion, minced
1 tablespoon mustard seeds
1 tablespoon grated baby ginger
½ cup white wine vinegar
½ cup dark beer
1¼ cups light brown sugar

1. Add the apples, raisins, onion, mustard seeds, and ginger to a large saucepan and cook gently until soft.

2. Add the vinegar, beer, and sugar, reduce the heat to low, and cook for 2 to 3 hours. Remove from heat.

3. Transfer to an airtight container. Refrigerate until ready to serve.

Sauteed Perpetual Spinach Scented with Nutmeg

MAKES 4 SERVINGS

Although it's not actually spinach, it's practically "perpetual" at West Haven Farm, available at the market stand most of the year. This biennial heirloom chard dating back to the 1860s has huge, shiny green leaves that are very similar to true spinach in terms of taste and texture. If anything, it's slightly milder in flavor, so in this dish it benefits from the sweetness and warmth of freshly grated nutmeg.

1½ pounds West Haven Farm
   Perpetual Spinach
2 tablespoons extra-virgin olive oil
1 whole nutmeg

1. Discard blemished spinach leaves and tough stems. Rinse the spinach and drain well.

2. Heat the oil in a large skillet. Add the spinach. Cook over medium heat, stirring rapidly, just until the spinach begins to wilt, about 1 minute. Remove from heat.

3. Transfer to a warmed serving dish. Grate about ¼ of the nutmeg over top and pass family style around the table.

MAIN DISHES

Coq au Vin Blanc (Chicken in Chardonnay)

MAKES 4 SERVINGS

Savory, comforting, and quintessentially French, coq au vin is cooked with red wine, a bottle of burgundy by tradition. In this market-inspired recipe, white wine, a lightly oaked Treleaven chardonnay, is swapped for red, resulting in brighter, livelier flavors. Serve with "Aglio e Olio" Mashed Potatoes (see page 130).

Jasper Meadows Farm is a two-person operation. Chuck and Madi butcher in small batches of no more than fifty free-range birds, for the health of the land, the birds, and themselves. "We care about the critters before they become your food," explains Madi. "Eating is a transfer of energy, and you want that energy to be as positive and loved as possible."

1 tablespoon olive oil

1 whole Jasper Meadows Farm chicken, cut into 2 drumsticks, 2 thighs, 2 wings, and 2 breasts

kosher salt

freshly ground black pepper

8 ounces white pearl onions, blanched 3 minutes and peeled

1 medium Valley View Farm Candy onion, finely chopped

¼ cup finely chopped celery

4 cloves garlic, sliced

9 ounces Wellspring Forest Farm oyster mushrooms, trimmed

1 cup Treleaven Tacie's Chardonnay

1 tablespoon lemon juice

2 tablespoons unsalted butter

1. Heat the oil on medium-high in a 4-quart stovetop casserole or saute pan.

2. Add half of the chicken pieces, skin side down. Cook until lightly browned, season with salt and pepper, and turn to brown the other side. Remove to a platter and repeat with remaining chicken.

3. Add pearl onions to the pan and toss until lightly browned. Remove to a dish.

4. Reduce heat to low. Add the chopped onion, celery, and garlic, cook until softened, and stir in the mushrooms. Add the wine, bring to a simmer, and season with salt, pepper, and lemon juice.

5. Return chicken to pan with any accumulated juices, baste, cover, and cook, about 30 minutes, basting a few more times. Remove the chicken to a platter.

6. Increase heat to medium-high and cook the sauce and mushrooms until sauce thickens, about 5 to 6 minutes. Lower heat and add the pearl onions and butter.

7. Return chicken to pan, baste and simmer, about 2 to 3 minutes. Remove from heat.

8. Transfer chicken and sauce to a deep, warmed platter and pass family style around the table.

Kohlrabi Latkes

MAKES 3 DOZEN LATKES

Before the potato, latkes were, and in some places still are, made from a variety of other vegetables. Grating and quick cooking brings out the lovely sweet-but-peppery flavor of West Haven Farm's organically grown kohlrabi, as it takes the form of these crispy, savory pancakes. Serve with Cherry Tomato Confit (see page 47).

3 West Haven Farm kohlrabi bulbs, peeled completely
1 medium Valley View Farm Candy onion, peeled and cut into quarters
2 large eggs
½ cup all-purpose flour
2 teaspoons kosher salt
1 teaspoon baking powder
½ teaspoon freshly ground black pepper
vegetable oil, for frying

1. Grate the kohlrabi and onion using the shredding disk of a food processor. Place shredded vegetables in a piece of cheesecloth and wring, extracting as much moisture as possible.

2. Place the shredded, drained kohlrabi and onion into a medium bowl. Add the eggs, flour, salt, baking powder, and pepper, and mix until the flour is absorbed.

3. Heat ¼ inch of oil in a large, heavy-bottomed skillet over medium-high heat. Place heaping spoonfuls of kohlrabi mixture into the hot oil, pressing down to form ¼- to ½-inch-thick patties. Cook until golden brown, 4 to 5 minutes. Flip and repeat on the other side. Transfer latkes to paper towels to drain.

4. Arrange on a warmed platter and serve any additional desired toppings such as sour cream or applesauce.

Sole "Bonne Femme" with Oyster Mushrooms

MAKES 4 SERVINGS

"No meal is ever dull when there is wine to drink and talk about," writes Andre Simon, founder of the Wine and Food Society.

French for "good wife," bonne femme describes a dish prepared in an uncomplicated, homey manner. In this market-inspired notion of a French country classic, the refined flavor of sole is married with a generous portion of briny oyster mushrooms from Wellspring Forest Farm and poached in an unoaked Treleaven chardonnay from King Ferry Winery. Besides sole, try the preparation with flounder, haddock, halibut, or cod. For perfect compatibility with the dish, serve the remainder of the chardonnay and uncork a second bottle.

1½ teaspoons unsalted butter
¼ pound Wellspring Forest Farm oyster mushrooms, thinly sliced
2 shallots, minced
⅓ cup Treleaven Silver Lining Chardonnay
sea salt
freshly ground black pepper
4 sole fillets, rinsed and dried
chives, chopped into chiffonade

1. In a wide saute pan set over medium heat, melt butter and saute mushrooms, about 4 to 5 minutes. Add shallots and wine and season with salt and pepper to taste.

2. Lower the heat, add the sole fillets, and simmer, about 10 minutes or until the fish flakes easily with a fork. Remove from heat.

3. To serve, arrange the fillets in the center of each of 4 warmed dinner plates and spoon mushrooms and pan juices around each serving and scatter chives over the top.

DESSERT

Toasted Walnut Farm Cookies

MAKES 1 DOZEN COOKIES

Richard Sabol planted three walnut trees on the Sabol family farm twenty-five years ago. With his care and attention, each tree may yield up to 20 pounds of walnuts in a single year.

These buttery, nutty cookies are all about the walnuts. Toasting walnuts adds a richer, deeper flavor to the moist, flaky texture. Note: if you don't have a nutcracker, place each walnut on a flat surface. With the pointy end facing up, gently strike the walnut with a hammer. As the shell cracks open along the axis, pull apart.

1½ cups shelled and coarsely chopped
   Sabol's Farm walnuts
1 tablespoon olive oil
1¼ cups all-purpose flour
½ cup white sugar
½ cup packed brown sugar
¼ teaspoon baking soda
1 Kingbird Farm chicken egg
1 teaspoon vanilla extract
½ cup butter, softened

1. Preheat oven to 375 degrees F. On a baking sheet lined with foil, toss walnuts in oil. Arrange in a single layer and toast until browned and fragrant, stirring occasionally, about 5 to 7 minutes. Remove from oven and set aside.

2. Grease a large cookie sheet.

3. In a medium bowl, stir together the flour, both sugars, and baking soda. Add the egg, vanilla, and butter and mix to form a dough. Stir in the walnuts.

4. Roll dough into 1-inch balls and place 2 inches apart onto the prepared cookie sheet.

5. Bake about 8 to 10 minutes, until golden brown. Remove from oven.

6. Allow cookies to cool on the baking sheet briefly before removing to a wire rack to cool completely.

7. Store in an airtight container until ready to serve.

ACKNOWLEDGMENTS

Our thanks to Monika Roth, retired agriculture educator at Cornell Cooperative Extension and adviser to the market; Max Buckner, president of the market board; Kelly Sauve, market organizational manager; Carrie Cuinn, market operations manager; Steve Sierigk, retired commissioner of the rutabaga curl; Dennis Hayes, champion of all things Upstate New York; and special thanks to Jake Bonar of North Country Books for his encouragement and support.

Special thanks to those who contributed historical photographs of the market throughout the years:

Allison Usavage

Lucy Bergstrom

Jan Norman

Steve Gibian

Dede Hatch

Stephen Singer

Amy Hnatko

Noelia Springston

Monika Roth

PARTICIPATING VENDORS

Bellwether Hard Cider

Berkshire Hills Honey Bee Farm

Black Diamond Farm

Blackduck Cidery

Bright Raven Apiary

Buried Treasures Organic Farm

Cayuta Sun Farm

Crosswinds Creamery

Damiani Wine Cellars

Daring Drake Farm

Dirtbaby Farm

Ely Fruit Farms

Eve's Cidery

Fort Baptist Farm

Forty Weight Roasters

Glenhaven Farm

Glenwood Farms

Humble Hill Farm

Jackman Vineyards

Jasper Meadows Farm

Just a Few Acres Farm

Kingbird Farm

King Ferry Winery

Knapp Farm

Littletree Orchards

Main Street Farm

Mandeville Farm

Mushroom Spirits Distillery

New York Cider Company

Nook & Cranny Farm

Old Chatham Creamery

Oxbow Farm

Picaflor Farm

Rainbow Valley Ranch

Redbyrd Orchard

Sabol's Farm

Schoolyard Sugarbush

Shagbark Gardens

Shannon Brock Farm

Six Circles Farm

Snow Farm Creamery

Stick and Stone Farm

Straight-Way Farm

Valley View Farm

Waid's Apiaries

Wellspring Forest Farm

West Haven Farm

Wide Awake Bakery

MARKET INGREDIENT INDEX

garlic
German Red, 94, 112, 142
Music, 102
Spanish Roja, 47, 49, 53, 54, 55, 56, 70, 73, 96, 99, 100, 103, 106, 107, 109, 113, 130, 131, 134, 139
garlic greens, 9
garlic scapes, 51, 74
grape juice, 90

Hakurei turnips, 10
honey
basswood, 116
buckwheat, 91, 138
goldenrod, 124
Japanese knotweed, 125
spring, 10, 11
summer, 80
wildflower, 6, 20, 38, 55, 162

kale
curly, 53, 55, 132
Red Russian, 139
Tuscan, 96, 107, 113
White Russian, 139
kale raab, 12
kohlrabi, 169
komatsuna, 16

leeks, 144

maple syrup, 20, 108, 116, 126, 134
milk, 11, 20, 42, 77, 79, 108, 110, 127, 134, 136, 143
mushrooms, 168, 170

okra, 59
onions, 16, 19, 21, 48, 50, 52, 62, 72, 107, 113, 134, 142, 144, 168, 169

pak choi, 14
parsnips, 142, 143, 144
peaches, 80
pears, 82
peppers
Italian sweet, 48, 73, 96
jalapeno, 52, 56, 62

serrano, 52, 62, 72
shishito, 45
popping corn, 64
potatoes
Abundance, 44
Keuka Gold, 8, 97, 130, 136, 142
Nicola, 163
pumpkins, 110

radishes
daikon, 21
Easter egg, 10
French breakfast, 22
ramps, 15
rhubarb, 5, 21, 30
rutabaga, 134

sorrel, 8
spinach,
Kolibri, 103
perpetual, 166
Space, 61
stinging nettles, 19
strawberries
Dickens, 72
Jewel, 42
sunchokes, 27
sweet potatoes, 94, 142

tatsoi, 21, 94
tomatillos, 62, 70
tomatoes
cherry, mixed, 39, 47, 73
heirloom, mixed, 46, 52, 63, 113
turnips, 136, 144

vodka, 158
walnuts, 107, 116, 146, 172

wine
cabernet franc, 82, 162
chardonnay, 168, 170
Riesling, 24, 107
Vino Bianco, 28

zucchini, 65, 74, 113

PARTICIPATING VENDOR INDEX

ABOUT THE AUTHORS AND PHOTOGRAPHER

A pioneer localist, **Michael Turback** created and nurtured an Ithaca institution, one of Upstate New York's first destination restaurants, built on his ability to stalk, procure, and support the best of local food and wine. The *Los Angeles Times* called Turback's of Ithaca "the first Finger Lakes restaurant to really devote itself to New York's culinary and enological bounty."

Besides an extraordinary appreciation of local bounty, Michael is well-informed and patriotically enthusiastic about all things Finger Lakes, and he knows the region inside and out.

In a review of his well-researched book, *Greetings from the Finger Lakes: A Food and Wine Lover's Companion*, Kevin Zraly, founder of the Windows on the World Wine School, wrote: "Michael Turback has captured the region's personality with his own passion for food and wine."

Michael is the author of the original *Ithaca Farmers Market Cookbook*. He has also produced cookbooks for the North Market in Columbus, Ohio, and the Findlay Market in Cincinnati, Ohio.

Just like the ingredients in this cookbook, **Izzy Lecek** is locally grown. Born and raised in Ithaca, she has been invested in foodways from a young age. During high school, she worked at the Ithaca Youth Farm Project, a community engagement and food justice program, building leadership, teamwork, and communication skills through a farming experience.

Professionally, she began her career at Moosewood, Ithaca's beloved vegetarian restaurant, then worked as baker for Macro Mamas, creating vegan desserts for the Ithaca Farmers Market.

Cocreating this book has instilled a deep understanding of the benefits of cooking with fresh, seasonal produce. This work is a love letter to her hometown and its vibrant food community.

Commercial and editorial photographer **Robyn Wishna** has been practicing her art for decades, capturing the complexity of many subjects and translating them back to the viewer with a fresh, genuine aesthetic. Her work for this book is a follow-up to her photos in the 2010 *Ithaca Farmers Market Cookbook*.

Her portrait project, "Spirit of Tompkins," was a collaboration with the town of Ithaca and the Discovery Trail, photographing and videotaping more than one hundred people and groups across the county. For "We Are Ithaca," she photographed more than twelve hundred local people in pop-up photo studios around the city.

Wishna has photographed kitchens, farms, and vineyards around the Finger Lakes for *Edible Finger Lakes* magazine and *Fresh Dirt* magazine, where she served as photo editor.